cables & arans

THE HARMONY GUIDES

cables & arans

250 stitches to knit

edited by Erika Knight

INTERWEAVE PRESS.
interweavebooks.com

First published in the United States by
Interweave Press LLC
201 East Fourth Street
Loveland, CO 80537-5655
Interweavebooks.com

Library of Congress Cataloging-in-Publication Data

Harmony guides. Cables and arans : 250 stitches to knit / Erika Knight,
editor.
        p. cm.
   Includes index.
   ISBN 978-1-59668-058-6 (pbk.)
   1. Knitting--Patterns. I. Knight, Erika.
   TT825.H39723 2007
   746.43'2041--dc22
                              2007023296

ISBN-13: 978-1-59668-058-6
ISBN-10: 1-59668-058-X

CIP data has been applied for with the Library of Congress

10 9 8 7 6 5 4 3 2

Reproduction by Dot Gradations Ltd
Printed and bound by SNP Leefung Printers Ltd, China

contents

inspiration

Cables and Arans are traditionally romantic, rugged and instantly recognizable; they create the most wonderful surface interest and scale to any knitted fabric.

The *Harmony Stitch Guides* are at the heart of every knitter's craft, an essential Bible; reference book, resource manual, and companion! A fountain of knitting knowledge, they are an authorative collection of creating knitted fabrics, from the simple to the intricate.

As a knitwear designer, the Harmony guides have been my mentor, my support, and often my inspiration. Always at hand, they frequently solve the problem and always spark an idea! However, it's often frustrating having to flick through pages of ribs, cables, woven, or Aran stitches, when you are just looking for a pretty lace or eyelet pattern, hoping to find more. This has certainly been my experience, and so I was delighted to be given the opportunity to edit this wonderful library of stitches into an easily accessible collection of distinctive stitch titles—your one-stop shop!

I like to keep things simple, so this new collection is your quintessential guide to browse through or dip in and out of, but always there for you when you need it!

I also couldn't resist scooping up old favorites—tried, tested and trusted stitches—as well as experimenting with a few more to add some extras to each title.

Whether you are an accomplished knitter or just thinking about picking up needles for the first time, there is something for every skill level—from starter to specialist. Everyone who is passionate about knitting will find inspiration and technical know-how within these pages.

The intricate patterns and history of Aran knitting have been a constant fascination for me. The Aran Isles, (Inishmore, Inishmaan, and Inisheer)—from which the knitting gets its name—lie off the west coast of Ireland in the storm-washed mouth of Galway Bay. This harsh environment required the wearing of warm and practical clothing for protection in the daily toil of farming and fishing and Aran sweaters were originally worn for outdoor work.

Traditionally made by men, who where adept at ropemaking—twisting, braiding, and folding the hemp—they took these shapes into the knitting of the yarn spun by the womenfolk, and the distinctive patterns have been recorded and handed down through the generations.

Aran sweaters were knitted in coarse, unscoured bainin (bawneen) wool, which retains its natural lanolin, making the garment more waterproof. The traditional creamy color is known as "biblical white."

The origins of Aran patterns reflect elements of Celtic culture and religion based on interlacing knots found on stone crosses and in the *Book of Kells*. One of the most popular stitches still used today is "The Trinity"—three stitches worked into one—representing the holy trinity.

The sweaters are characterized by a large central panel bordered by varying numbers of side panels on a textural background. Usually symmetrical, these side panels are knitted in simpler stitch patterns—a useful device for scaling up larger sizes. Even the welts, cuffs, and neckbands are worked with complex stitches to create highly decorative and unique textiles.

Arans came to the forefront of fashion in 1934 when pioneering documentary film maker Robert O'Flaherty made *Man of Aran*, dressing the cinema ushers in "Seamens Jerseys and Tam O'Shanters". Textile journalist Heinz Kiewe, who did much to preserve Irish country crafts, bought back a sweater from a crafts cooperative and showed it to fashion journalist Mary Thomas. As Britain emerged from austerity during the late 1940s, Aran sweaters became very popular. In 1956, *Vogue* magazine featured an Aran and by the late 1950s they had caught on in America.

Arans are forever popular, both on the catwalk and for individual knitters who love to create the challenging sculpted effects, but the rich combination of stitches and textures can take on an even more exciting contemporary look when worked in mohair, lurex, cotton, denim, or colored yarns. The techniques involved will require a little practice, but once mastered, the twisting, crossing, cabling, and bobbling will keep you challenged and absorbed!

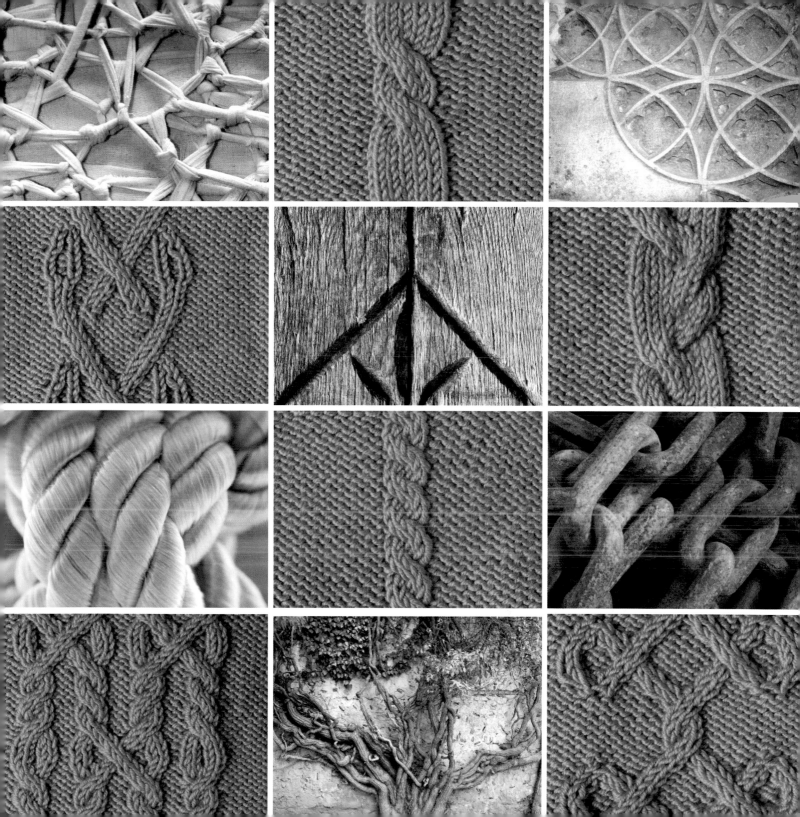

tools & equipment

To master any skill, it's imperative to have a solid foundation of the techniques. This section provides useful information that can come in handy while knitting.

Knitting needles

Knitting needles are used in pairs to produce a flat knitted fabric. They are pointed at one end to form the stitches and have a knob at the other to retain the stitches. They may be made in plastic, wood, steel, or alloy and range in size from 2mm to 17mm in diameter. In England, needles used to be sized by numbers—the higher the number, the smaller the needle. In America, the opposite is true—higher numbers indicate larger sizes. Metric sizing has now been internationally adopted. Needles are also made in different lengths that will comfortably hold the stitches required for each project.

It is useful to have a range of sizes so that gauge swatches can be knitted up and compared. Discard any needles that become bent. Points should be fairly sharp; blunt needles reduce the speed and ease of working.

Circular and double-pointed needles are used to produce a tubular fabric or flat rounds. Many traditional fisherman's sweaters are knitted in the round. Double-pointed needles are sold in sets of four or five. Circular needles consist of two needles joined by a flexible length of plastic. The plastic varies in length. Use the shorter lengths for knitting sleeves, neckbands etc, and the longer lengths for larger pieces such as sweaters and skirts.

Cable needles are short needles used to hold the stitches of a cable to the back or front of the main body of knitting.

Needle gauges are punched with holes corresponding to the needles sizes and are marked with both the old numerical sizing and the metric sizing so you can easily check the size of any needle.

Stitch holders resemble large safety pins and are used to hold stitches while they are not being worked, for example, around a neckline when the neckband stitches will be picked up and worked after back and front have been joined. As an alternative, thread a blunt-pointed sewing needle with a generous length of contrast-colored yarn, thread it through the stitches to be held while they are still on the needles, then slip the stitches off the needles and knot both ends of the contrast yarn to secure the stitches.

Wool sewing needles or tapestry needles are used to sew completed pieces of knitting together. They are large with a broad eye for easy threading and a blunt point that will slip between the knitted stitches with out splitting and fraying the yarn. Do not use the sharp-pointed sewing needles to sew up knitting.

A row counter is used to count the number of rows that have been knitted. It is a cylinder with a numbered dial that is pushed onto the needles and the dial is turned at the completion of each row.

A tape measure is essential for checking the tension swatches and for measuring the length and width of completed knitting. For an accurate result, always smooth the knitting (without stretching) on a firm flat surface before measuring it.

A crochet hook is useful for picking up dropped stitches.

Knitting Yarn

Yarn is the term used for strands of spun fiber which are twisted together into a continuous length of the required thickness. Yarn can be of animal origin (wool, angora, mohair, silk, alpaca), vegetable origin (cotton, linen), or man-made (nylon, acrylic, rayon). Knitting yarn may be made up from a combination of different fibers.

Each single strand of yarn is known as a ply. A number of plys are twisted together to form the yarn. The texture and characteristics of the yarn may be varied by the combination of fibers and by the way in which the yarn is spun. Wool and other natural fibers are often combined with man-made fibers to make a yarn that is more economical and hard-wearing. Wool can also be treated to make it machine washable. The twist of the yarn is firm and smooth and knits up into a hard-wearing fabric. Loosely twisted yarn has a softer finish when knitted.

Buying Yarn

Yarn is most commonly sold wound into balls of specific weight measured into grams or ounces. Some yarn, particularly very thick yarn, is also sold in a coiled hank or skein that must be wound into a ball before you can begin knitting.

Yarn manufacturers (called spinners) wrap each ball with a paper band on which is printed a lot of necessary information. The ball band states the weight of the yarn and its composition. It will give instructions for the washing and ironing and will state the ideal range of needle sizes to be used with the yarn. The ball band also carries the shade number and dye lot number. It is important that you use yarn of the same dye lot for an entire project. Different dye lots vary subtly in shading that may not be apparent when you are holding the two balls, but which will show as a variation in shade on the finished piece of knitting.

Always keep the ball band as a reference. The best way is to pin it to the gauge swatch (see page 17) and keep them together with any left over yarn and spare buttons or other trimmings. That way you can always check the washing instructions and also have materials for repairs.

the basics

Once you have mastered the basics of knitting; you can go on to develop your skills and start making more challenging projects.

Casting On

1 Make a slip knot 39in (1m) from the end of the yarn. Hold the needle in your right hand with the ball end of the yarn over your index finger. Wind the loose end of the yarn around your left thumb from front to back.

2 Insert the point of the needle under the first strand of yarn on your thumb.

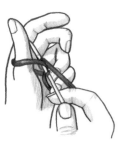

3 With your right index finger, take the ball end of the yarn over the point of the needle.

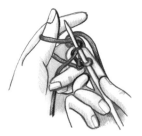

4 Pull a loop through to form the first stitch. Remove your left thumb from the yarn. Pull the loose end to secure the stitch. Repeat until all stitches have been cast on.

Knit Stitch

1 Hold the needle with the cast-on stitches in your left hand, with the loose yarn at the back of the work. Insert the right-hand needle from the left to right through the front of the first stitch on the left-hand needle.

2 Wind the yarn from left to right over the point of the right-hand needle.

3 Draw the yarn through the stitch, thus forming a new stitch on the right-hand needle.

4 Slip the original stitch off the left-hand needle, keeping the new stitch on the right-hand needle.

5 To knit a row, repeat steps 1 to 4 until all the stitches have been transferred from the left-hand needle to the right-hand needle. Turn the work, transferring the needle with the stitches to your left hand to work the next row.

Purl Stitch

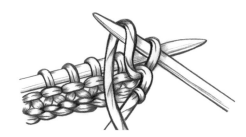

I Hold the needle with the stitches in your left hand with the loose yarn at the front of the work. Insert the right-hand needle from right to left into the front of the front of the first stitch on the left-hand needle.

2 Wind the yarn from right to left over the point of the right-hand needle.

3 Draw the yarn through the stitch, thus forming a new stitch on the right-hand needle.

4 Slip the original stitch off the left-hand needle, keeping the new stitch on the right-hand needle.

5 To purl a row, repeat steps 1 to 4 until all the stitches have been transferred from the left-hand needle to the right-hand needle. Turn the work, transferring the needle with the stitches to your left hand to work the next row.

Increasing

The simplest method of increasing one stitch is to work into the front and back of the same stitch.

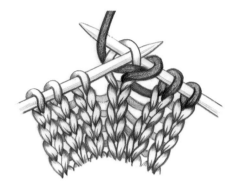

On a knit row, knit into the front of the stitch to be increased, then before slipping it off the needle, place the right-hand needle behind the left-hand needle and knit again into the back of the same stitch. Slip the original stitch off the left-hand needle.

On a purl row, purl into the front of the stitch to be increased, then before slipping it off the needle, purl again into the back of the same stitch. Slip the original stitch off the left-hand needle.

Decreasing

The simplest method of decreasing one stitch is to work two stitches together.

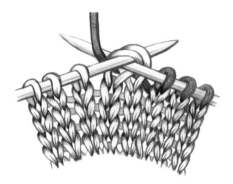

On a knit row, insert the right-hand needle from left to right through two stitches instead of one, then knit them together as one stitch. This is called knit two together (k2tog).

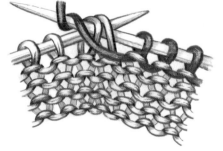

On a purl row, insert the right-hand needle from right to left through two stitches instead of one, then purl them together as one stitch. This is called purl two together (p2tog).

Binding Off

There is one simple, most commonly used method of securing stitches once you have finished a piece of knitting —binding off. The bind-off edge should always have the same "give" or elasticity as the fabric and you should always bind off in the stitch pattern used for the main fabric, unless the pattern directs otherwise.

Knitwise

Knit two stitches. *Using the point of the left-hand needle lift the first stitch on the right-hand needle over the second then drop it off the needle. Knit the next stitch and repeat from * until all stitches have been worked off the left-hand needle and only one stitch remains on the right-hand needle. Cut the yarn (leaving enough to sew in the end), thread the end through the stitch then slip it off the needle. Draw the yarn up firmly to fasten off.

Purlwise

Purl two stitches. *Using the point of the left-hand needle, lift the first stitch on the right-hand needle over the second and drop it off the needle. Purl the next stitch and repeat from * until all the stitches have been worked off the left-hand needle and only one stitch remains on the right-hand

needle. Secure the last stitch as described in binding off knitwise.

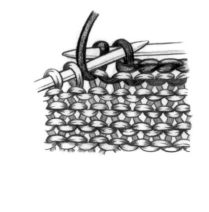

The excitement of arriving at the last stage of your knitting can make you bind off without the same care that you have used in the rest of the work. You should take into account the part of the garment you are working on. If it is a neckband, you need to make sure that your bind-off edge is not too tight, preventing the neck from going over the wearer's head. If you are a tight knitter, you may need to bind off with a larger needle. Most neckbands or frontbands on a jacket or cardigan are worked in rib and should be bound off "ribwise" by knitting the knit stitches and purling the purl stitches as you bind off along the row. Lace stitches should also be bound off in pattern, slipping, making stitches, or decreasing as you go to make sure that the fabric doesn't widen or gather up.

Gauge (or tension)

The correct gauge (or tension) is the most important contribution to the successful knitting of a garment. The information under this heading given at the beginning of all patterns refers to the number of stitches required to fill a particular area; for example, a frequent gauge indication would be "22sts and 30 rows = 4in (10cm) square measured over stockinette stitch on size 6 (4mm) needles." This means that it is necessary to produce fabric made up of the proportion of stitches and rows as given in the gauge paragraph in order to obtain the correct measurements for the garment you intend to knit, regardless of the needles you use. The needle size indicated in the pattern is the one which most knitters will use to achieve this gauge, but it is the gauge, that is important, not needle size.

The way to ensure that you do achieve the correct gauge is to work a gauge sample or swatch before starting the main part of the knitting. Although this may seem to be time wasting and a nuisance, it can save the enormous amount of time and aggravation that would result from having knitted a garment the wrong size.

Gauge Swatch

The instructions given in the gauge paragraph of a knitting pattern are either for working in stockinette stitch or in pattern stitch. If they are given in pattern stitch, it is necessary to work a multiple of stitches the same as the multiple required in the pattern. If it's in stockinette stitch, any number can be cast on, but whichever method is used should always be at least 5in (12cm) in width. Work in pattern or stockinette stitch according to the wording of the gauge paragraph until the piece measures at least 4in (10cm) in depth. Break the yarn about 6in (15cm) from the work and thread this end through the stitches, then remove the knitting needle. Place a pin vertically into the fabric a few

stitches from the side edge. Measure 4in (10cm) carefully and insert a second pin. Count the stitches. If the number of stitches between the pins is less than that specified in the pattern (even by half a stitch) your garment will be too large. Use smaller needles and knit another gauge sample. If your sample has more stitches over 4in (10cm), the garment will be too small. Change to larger needles. Check the number of rows against the given gauge also.

It is most important to get the width measurement correct before starting to knit. Length measurements can usually be adjusted during the course of the knitting by adjusting the measurements to underarm or sleeve length, which is frequently given as a measurement and not in rows

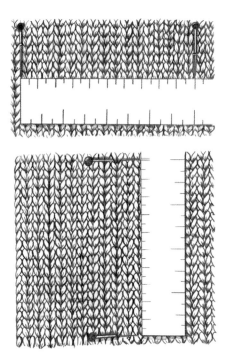

How to Read Charts

Charts are read exactly as the knitting is worked—from the bottom to the top. After the last row at the top has been worked, repeat the sequence from row 1.

Each symbol represents an instruction. Symbols have been designed to resemble the actual appearance of the knitting. This is more difficult to do with multi-color slip-stitch patterns that have to be knitted before the mosaic effects become obvious.

Before starting to knit, look up all the symbols on your chosen chart so that you are familiar with the techniques involved. These may be shown with the pattern as a special abbreviation. The most common abbreviations that are not shown as special abbreviations will be given at the bottom of each page. Make sure you understand the difference between working similar symbols on a right-side and a wrong-side row. Before working a particular pattern, it is important to read the relevant information.

Each square represents a stitch and each horizontal line represents a row. Place a ruler above the line you are working and work the symbols one by one. If you are new to chart reading, try comparing the charted instructions with the written ones.

For knitters who wish to follow the written directions, it is still a good idea to look at the chart (where available) before starting, to see what the repeat looks like and how the pattern had been balanced.

Right-Side and Wrong-Side Rows

"Right-side rows" are rows where the right side of the fabric is facing you when you work, and "wrong-side rows" are rows where the wrong is facing you when you work. Row numbers are shown at the side of the charts at the beginning of the row. Right-side rows are always read from right to left. Wrong-side rows are always read from left to right.

Symbols on charts are shown as they appear from the right side of the work. Therefore, a horizontal dash strands for a purl "bump" on the right side, regardless of whether it was achieved by purling on a right-side row or knitting on a wrong-side row. To make things clearer, symbols for right-side rows are slightly darker than those for wrong-side rows.

Pattern Repeats and Multiples

The "Multiple" or repeat of the pattern is given with each set of instructions, for example "Multiple of 7 + 4." This means you can cast on any number of stitches that is a multiple of 7, plus 4 balancing stitches. For instance, 14 + 4, 21 + 4, 28 + 4, etc.

In the written instructions, the 7 stitches are shown in parentheses or brackets or follow an asterisk *, and these stitches are repeated across the row the required number of times. In charted instructions, the pattern repeat is contained between heavier vertical lines. The extra stitches not included in the pattern repeat are there to "balance" the row or make it symmetrical and are only worked once.

Some patterns require a foundation row that is worked once before commencing the pattern but does not form part of the repeat. On charts, this row is marked by a letter "F" and is separated from the pattern repeat by a heavier horizontal line.

stitch gallery

Small Cable with Grooves

Multiple of 12.

1st row (right side): *K2, p1, k6, p1, k2; rep from * to end.

2nd row: *P2, k1, p6, k1, p2; rep from * to end.

3rd, 5th, 7th, and 9th rows: *K2, p2, k4, p2, k2; rep from * to end.

4th, 6th, and 8th rows: *P2, k2, p4, k2, p2; rep from * to end.

10th row: *P2, slip next 2 sts onto cable needle and hold at front of work, p2, k2 from cable needle, slip next 2 sts onto cable needle and hold at front of work, k2, p2 from cable needle, p2; rep from * to end.

11th row: Knit.

12th row: As 2nd row.

Rep these 12 rows.

Baby Cable and Garter Ridges

Multiple of 25.

1st row (right side): *P9, k4, p12; rep from * to end.

2nd row: *[P3, k1] 3 times, p4, k1, [p3, k1] twice; rep from * to end.

3rd row: *[P1, k3] twice, p1, C4F, [p1, k3] 3 times; rep from * to end.

4th row: As 2nd row.

Rep these 4 rows.

Alternating Twists

Multiple of 9 + 2.

1st row (wrong side): K2, *p3, k1, p3, k2; rep from * to end.

2nd row: *P2, wyib sl 1, k2, p1, k2, wyib sl 1; rep from * to last 2 sts, p2.

3rd row: K2, *wyif sl 1, p2, k1, p2, wyif sl 1, k2; rep from * to end.

4th row: *P2, drop sl st off needle to front of work, k2, pick up dropped st and k it, p1, wyib sl next 2 sts, drop sl st off needle to front of work, sl same 2 sts back to LH needle, pick up dropped st and k it; rep from * to last 2 sts, p2.

5th row: K2, *p3, k1, p3, k2; rep from * to end.

6th row: *P2, k3, p1, k3; rep from * to last 2 sts, p2.

Rep these 6 rows.

Twists with Knotted Pattern

Multiple of 20.

1st row (right side): *P2, k5, p5, k5, p3; rep from * to end.

2nd and every alt row: *K3, p5, k5, p5, k2; rep from * to end.

3rd row: As 1st row.

5th row: *P2, using another ball of yarn k5, turn p5, work another 12 rows in St st on these 5 sts, place on stitch holder, slip next 5 sts onto cable needle and hold at back of work, using another ball of yarn k5, turn p5, work another 12 rows in St st on these 5 sts, place on stitch holder, knot the 2 strips as follows: put 2nd strip underneath 1st then over 1st, k5 sts from second strip, p5 sts from cable needle, k5 sts from first strip, p3; rep from * to end.

7th, 9th, 11th, 13th, and 15th rows: As 1st row.

16th row: As 2nd row.

Rep these 16 rows.

Alternated Twists

Multiple of 12.

1st row (right side): *P6, k6; rep from * to end.

2nd row: *P6, k6; rep from * to end.

3rd row: *P3, make 5 sts (pick up loop between next 2 sts and k1, p1, k1, p1, k1 into it), p3, C6F; rep from * to end.

4th row: *P6, k3, p5, k3; rep from * to end.

5th row: *P3, k5, p3, k6; rep from * to end.

6th, 8th, 10th, 12th, 14th, and 16th rows: As 4th row.

7th, 9th, 11th, 13th, and 15th rows: As 5th row.

17th row: *P3, bind off next 5 sts purlwise, (one st on RH needle) p2, C6F; rep from * to end.

18th row: *P6, k6; rep from * to end.

19th row: *K6, p6; rep from * to end.

20th row: *K6, p6; rep from * to end.

21st row: *C6F, p3, make 5, p3; rep from * to end.

22nd row: *K3, p5, k3, p6; rep from * to end.

23rd row: *K6, p3, k5, p3; rep from * to end.

24th, 26th, 28th, and 30th rows: As 22nd row.

25th, 27th, and 29th rows: As 23rd row.

31st row: *C6F, p3, bind off next 5 sts purlwise, p2; rep from * to end.

32nd row: *K6, p6; rep from * to end.

Rep these 32 rows.

Sand Wind

Multiple of 12 + 6 + 1 st for the rim on each edge.

1st (right side) & 5th row: Knit.

2nd row and all even rows: Purl.

3rd row: 1 edge st, *C6F, k6; rep from * to last st, 1 edge st.

7th row: 1 edge st, *k6, C6B; rep from * to last st, 1 edge st.

8th row: Knit.

Rep these 8 rows.

Rhombus

Panel of 12 sts on a St st background.

1st (right side) and 5th rows: Knit.

2nd row and all even rows: Purl.

3rd row: C4B, k4, C4F.

7th row: K2, C4F, C4B, k2.

8th row: Purl.

Rep these 8 rows.

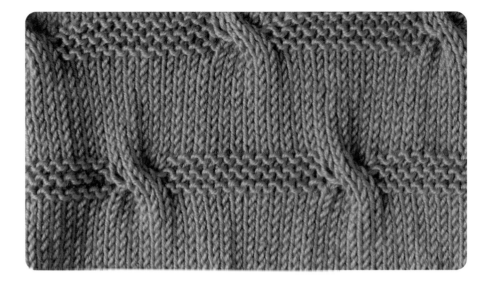

Twisted candles

Multiple of 18 + 8 + 1 st for the rim on each edge.

1st row (right side): Knit.

2nd row: Purl.

3rd and 5th rows: Knit.

4th row: Purl.

6th row: 1 edge st, k1, p6, k1, *k11, p6, k1; rep from * to last st, 1 edge st.

7th row: Knit.

8th row: As 6th row.

9th row: 1 edge st, *k1, C6F, k11; rep from * to last 9 sts, k1, C6F, k1, 1 edge st.

10th row: As 6th row.

11th to 21st rows: As 1st and 2nd rows.

22nd row: 1 edge st, *k10, p6, k10; rep from * to last st, 1 edge st.

23rd row: As 1st row.

24th row: As 22nd row.

25th row: 1 edge st *k10, c6f, k10; rep from * to last st, 1 edge st.

26th row: As 22nd row.

Rep these 26 rows.

Geometric Twisted Candles

Multiple of 10 + 6 + 1 st for the rim on each edge.

1st row (right side): 1 edge st, *p1, k4, p5;
rep from * to last 7 sts, p1, k4, p1, 1 edge st.

2nd row and all even rows: Knit all k sts and purl all p sts.

3rd row: Knit all k sts and purl all p sts.

5th row: 1 edge st, *p1, C4B, p5; rep from * to last 6 sts, p1, C4B, 1 edge st.

7th row: As 3rd row.

9th row: 1 edge st, *p6, k4; rep from * to last 7 sts, p6, 1 edge st

11th row: As 3rd row.

13th row: 1 edge st *p6, C4B; rep from * to last 7 sts, p6, 1 edge st.

15th row: As 3rd row.

16th row: As 2nd row.

Rep these 16 rows.

Crossed Grooves

Multiple of 8 + 2 + 1 st for the rim on each edge.

1st, 3rd, 5th, 9th, 11th, and 13th rows (right side): 1 edge st *k2, p2; rep from * to last 3 sts, k2, 1 edge st.

2nd row and all even rows: Knit all k sts and purl all p sts.

7th row: 1 edge st, *C6 (slip next 4 sts onto cable needle and hold at back of work, k2, slip 3rd and 4th st from cable needle onto left hand needle, p2tbl, k2 sts from cable needle), p2; rep from * to last 3 sts, k2, 1edge st.

15th row: 1 edge st, k2, *p2, C6; rep from * to last st, 1 edge st.

16th row: As 2nd row.

Rep these 16 rows.

20-Stitch Twisted Candle

Panel of 20 sts on a reverse St st background.

1st row (right side), 5th, 7th, 9th, and 11th rows: Knit.

2nd row and all even rows: Purl.

3rd row: C10b, C10f.

12th row: As 2nd row.

Rep these 12 rows.

Big Twisted Candle

Panel of 9 sts on a reverse St st background.

1st row (right side): Knit.

2nd row and all even rows: Purl.

3rd, 5th, 7th, 11th, 13th, 15th, and 17th rows: Knit.

9th row: C9 (slip next 4 sts onto cable needle and hold at front of work), k5, k4 from cable needle.

18th row: As 2nd row.

Rep these 18 rows.

Sloping Diamonds

Multiple of 10.

1st row (right side): *K2, p5, C3B; rep from * to end.

2nd row: *P3, k5, p2; rep from * to end.

3rd row: *K2, p4, C3B, k1; rep from * to end.

4th row: *P4, k4, p2; rep from * to end.

5th row: *K2, p3, T3B, k2; rep from * to end.

6th row: *P2, k1, p2, k3, p2; rep from * to end.

7th row: *K2, p2, T3B, p1, k2; rep from * to end.

8th row: *P2, [k2, p2] twice; rep from * to end.

9th row: *K2, p1, T3B, p2, k2; rep from * to end.

10th row: *P2, k3, p2, k1, p2; rep from * to end.

11th row: *K2, T3B, p3, k2; rep from * to end.

12th row: *P2, k4, p4; rep from * to end.

13th row: *K1, T3B, p4, k2; rep from * to end.

14th row: *P2, k5, p3; rep from * to end.

15th row: *T3B, p5, k2; rep from * to end.

16th row: *P2, k6, p2; rep from * to end.

Rep these 16 rows.

Rhombus Delight

Multiple of 10.

1st row (right side): *P1, k1tbl, p1, k1tbl, p1, T2B, k1, T2F; rep from * to end.

2nd row: *P5, k1, p1tbl, k1, p1tbl, k1; rep from * to end.

3rd row: *P1, k1tbl, p1, k1tbl, p1, T2B, k1, T2F; rep from * to end.

4th row: *K1, p3, k2, p1tbl, k1, p1tbl, k1; rep from * to end.

5th row: *P1, k1tbl, p1, k1tbl, p2, (k 3rd st on left-hand needle, k 2nd st on left handle, k 1st st on left-hand needle, slip all 3 sts off together), p1; rep from * to end.

6th row: As 4th row.

Rep these 6 rows.

Open Honeycomb

Multiple of 4 + 1 st for the rim on each edge.

1st (right side) row: 1 edge st *T2B, T2F; rep from * to last st, 1 edge st.

2nd row and all even rows: Purl.

3rd and 7th rows: Knit.

5th row: 1 edge st, *T2F, T2B; rep from * to last st, 1 edge st; rep from * to end.

8th row: As 2nd row.

Rep these 8 rows.

Ray of Honey

Multiple of 4 + 1 st for the rim on each edge.

1st (right side) row: 1 edge st *T2B, T2F; rep from * to last st, 1 edge st.

2nd and 4th rows: Purl.

3rd row: 1 edge st, *T2F, T2B; rep from * to last st, 1 edge st.

Rep these 4 rows.

Arched Cables

Multiple of 24 + 2.

1st row (right side): Knit.

2nd row and all even rows: K1, p to last st, k1.

3rd row: K1, *C4B, k4, C4F; rep from * to last st, k1.

5th row: Knit.

7th row: K3, C4F, C4B, *k4, C4F, C4B; rep from * to last 3 sts, k3.

8th row: K1, p to last st, k1.

Rep these 8 rows.

Mock Cable Wide Rib

Multiple of 13 + 8.

1st row (wrong side): P8, *k1, p3, k1, p8; rep from * to end.

2nd row: K8, *p1, slip 2 sts, k 3rd st on LH needle, k 2nd st, then k 1st st, then sl all 3 sts off LH needle, p1, k8, rep from * to end.

Rep these 2 rows.

Dramatic Curves

Multiple of 47 sts on 1st row; 62 sts thereafter.

1st row (right side): P8, *[k1, p1] in each of next 5 sts, p8; rep from * to end.

2nd row: K8 *p10, place point of left-hand needle into the st below needle of the last knit st just worked, knit it together with the next st on left-hand needle, k7; rep from * to end.

3rd row: P8, *k10, p8; rep from * to end.

4th row: As 2nd row.

5th to 12th rows: Rep last 2 rows 4 times more.

13th row: P8, sl next 10 sts onto cable needle and hold at front, sl foll 8 sts onto cable needle and hold at back, k10, p8 from sts held on 2nd cable needle, k10 from sts held on first cable needle, p8, k10, p8.

14th row: As 2nd row.

15th to 24th rows: Rep rows 3 and 4, 5 times.

25th row: P8, k10, p8, sl next 10 sts onto cable needle and hold at back of work, sl foll 8 sts onto cable needle and also hold at back, k10, p8 from sts held on 2nd cable needle, k10 from sts held on first cable needle, p8.

26th row: As 2nd row.

Rep from 3rd to 26th row.

Floating Snake Pattern

Multiple of 10 + 5.

Special Abbreviations

3-st RC (3 st right cross): Sl 2 sts onto cable needle and hold to back, k1, k2 from cable needle.

3-st LC (3 st left cross): Sl 1 st onto cable needle and hold to front, k2, k1 from cable needle.

1st row (right side): *P2, k1, p2, k1tbl, 3-st RC, k1tbl; rep from * to last 5 sts, p2, k1, p2.

2nd and 4th rows: *K2, p1, k2, wyif sl 1, p3, wyif sl 1; rep from * to last 5 sts, k2, p1, k2.

3rd row: *P2, k1, p2, k1tbl, 3-st LC, k1tbl; rep from * to last 5 sts, p2, k1, p2.

Rep these 4 rows.

Centered Cables

Panel of 16 sts on a background of reverse St st.

Special Abbreviations

T8B rib (twist 8 Back rib) = slip next 4 sts onto cable needle and hold at back of work, k1, p2, k1 from left-hand needle, then k1, p2, k1 from cable needle.

T8F rib (Twist 8 Front rib) = slip next 4 sts onto cable needle and hold at front of work, k1, p2, k1 from left-hand needle, then k1, p2, k1 from cable needle.

1st row (right side): K1, p2, [k2, p2] 3 times, k1.

2nd row: P1, k2, [p2, k2] 3 times, p1.

3rd row: T8B rib, T8F rib.

4th row: As 2nd row.

5th to 14th rows: Rep 1st and 2nd rows 5 times.

15th row: T8F rib, T8B rib.

16th row: As 2nd row.

17th to 24th rows: Rep 1st and 2nd rows 4 times.

Rep these 24 rows.

Floating Leaves

Panel of 9 sts on a background of reverse St st.

1st row (right side): C2F, p7.

2nd row: K6, T2FW, p1.

3rd row: KB1, p1, C2F, p5.

4th row: K4, T2FW, p1, k1, p1.

5th row: [KB1, p1] twice, C2F, p3.

6th row: K2, T2FW, [p1, k1] twice, p1.

7th row: [KB1, p1] 3 times, C2F, p1.

8th row: T2FW, [p1, k1] 3 times, p1.

9th row: [KB1, p1] 4 times, KB1.

10th row: [P1, k1] 3 times, p1, T2FW.

11th row: P1, T2F, [p1, KB1] 3 times.

12th row: [P1, k1] twice, p1, T2FW, k2.

13th row: P3, T2F, [p1, KB1] twice.

14th row: P1, k1, p1, T2FW, k4.

15th row: P5, T2F, p1, KB1.

16th row: P1, T2FW, k6.

17th row: P7, C2B.

18th row: P1, T2BW, k6.

19th row: P5, C2B, p1, KB1.

20th row: P1, k1, p1, T2BW, k4.

21st row: P3, C2B, [p1, KB1] twice.

22nd row: [P1, k1] twice, p1, T2BW, k2.

23rd row: P1, C2B, [p1, KB1] 3 times.

24th row: [P1, k1] 3 times, p1, T2BW.

25th row: [KB1, p1] 4 times, KB1.

26th row: T2BW, [p1, k1] 3 times, p1.

27th row: [KB1, p1] 3 times, T2B, p1.

28th row: K2, T2BW, [p1, k1] twice, p1.

29th row: [KB1, p1] twice, T2B, p3.

30th row: K4, T2BW, p1, k1, p1.

31st row: KB1, p1, T2B, p5.

32nd row: K6, T2BW, p1.

Rep these 32 rows.

Ascending Fern

Panel of 18 sts on a background of reverse St st.

1st row (right side): P5, [C2B, p1] twice, C2F, p5.

2nd row: K5, *[PB1] twice, k1; rep from * twice more, k4.

3rd row: P4, T2B, k1, p1, C2B, p1, k1, T2F, p4.

4th row: K4, [PB1, k1] twice, [PB1] twice, [k1, PB1] twice, k4.

5th row: P3, T2B, [C2B, p1] twice, C2F, T2F, p3.

6th row: K3, PB1, k1, *[PB1] twice, k1; rep from * twice more, PB1, k3.

7th row: P2, [T2B] twice, k1, p1, C2B, p1, k1, [T2F] twice, p2.

8th row: K2, [PB1, k1] 3 times, [PB1] twice, [k1, PB1] 3 times, k2.

9th row: P1, [T2B] twice, [C2B, p1] twice, C2F, [T2F] twice, p1.

10th row: K1, [PB1, k1] twice, *[PB1] twice, k1; rep from * twice more, [PB1, k1] twice.

11th row: [T2B] 3 times, k1, p1, C2B, p1, k1, [T2F] 3 times.

12th row: [PB1, k1] 4 times, [PB1] twice, [k1, PB1] 4 times.

13th and 14th rows: As 9th and 10th rows.

15th and 16th rows: As 7th and 8th rows.

17th and 18th rows: As 5th and 6th rows.

19th and 20th rows: As 3rd and 4th rows.

21st and 22nd rows: As 1st and 2nd rows.

23rd row: P6, k1, p1, C2B, p1, k1, p6.

24th row: K6, PB1, k1, [PB1] twice, k1, PB1, k6.

25th row: P8, C2B, p8.

26th row: K8, [PB1] twice, k8.

27th row: P8, C2B, p8.

28th row: K8, [PB1] twice, k8.

Rep these 28 rows.

Gentle Cord Pattern

Panel of 18 sts on a background of reverse St st.

Special Abbreviation

Bind 2 = yarn over needle to make a st, p2, pass new st over the 2 purl sts.

1st row (right side): K2, p3, k2, p4, k2, p3, k2.

2nd row: Bind 2, k3, bind 2, k4, bind 2, k3, bind 2.

3rd row: T3F, p2, T3F, [p2, T3B] twice.

4th row: K1, bind 2, k3, bind 2, k2, bind 2, k3, bind 2, k1.

5th row: P1, T3F, p2, T3F, T3B, p2, T3B, p1.

6th row: K2, bind 2, k3, bind 2, p2, k3, bind 2, k2.

7th row: P2, T3F, p2, C4B, p2, T3B, p2.

8th row: K3, bind 2, k2, [bind 2] twice, k2, bind 2, k3.

9th row: P3, [T3F, T3B] twice, p3.

10th row: K4, p2, bind 2, k2, p2, bind 2, k4.

11th row: P4, C4F, p2, C4F, p4.

12th row: K4, [bind 2] twice, k2, [bind 2] twice, k4.

13th row: P3, [T3B, T3F] twice, p3.

14th row: K3, bind 2, k2, bind 2, p2, k2, bind 2, k3.

15th row: P2, T3B, p2, C4B, p2, T3F, p2.

16th row: K2, bind 2, k3, [bind 2] twice, k3, bind 2, k2.

17th row: P1, T3B, p2, T3B, T3F, p2, T3F, p1.

18th row: As 4th row.

19th row: T3B, p2, T3B, [p2, T3F] twice.

20th row: As 2nd row.

21st to 24th rows: Rep 1st and 2nd rows twice.

Rep these 24 rows.

Divided Circles

Multiple of 28 + 18.

1st row (right side): P6, k6, *p1, [k2, p4] 3 times, k6; rep from * to last 6 sts, p6.

2nd row: K6, p6, *k4, p14, k4, p6; rep from * to last 6 sts, k6.

3rd row: P4, T4B, k2, *[T4F, p2] twice, k2, [p2, T4B] twice, k2; rep from * to last 8 sts, T4F, p4.

4th row: K4, *p10, k4; rep from * to end.

5th row: P2, T4B, p2, k2, *[p2, T4F] twice, k2, [T4B, p2] twice, k2; rep from * to last 8 sts, p2, T4F, p2.

6th row: K2, p14, *k4, p6, k4, p14; rep from * to last 2 sts, k2.

7th row: P2, *[k2, p4] 3 times, k6, p4; rep from * to last 16 sts, k2, [p4, k2] twice, p2.

8th row: As 6th row.

9th row: P2, T4F, p2, k2, *[p2, T4B] twice, k2, [T4F, p2] twice, k2; rep from * to last 8 sts, p2, T4B, p2.

10th row: As 4th row.

11th row: P4, T4F, k2, *[T4B, p2] twice, k2, [p2, T4F] twice, k2; rep from * to last 8 sts, T4B, p4.

12th row: As 2nd row.

Rep these 12 rows.

8-Stitch Snakey Cable

Panel of 8 sts on a background of reverse St st.

1st row (right side): Knit.

2nd row: Purl.

3rd row: C8B.

4th row: Purl.

5th to 8th rows: Rep 1st and 2nd rows twice more.

9th row: C8F.

10th row: Purl.

11th and 12th rows: Rep 1st and 2nd rows once.

Rep these 12 rows.

Sloping Cable

Panel 10 sts on a background of reverse St st.

Note: Increases should be made by knitting into front and back of next st.

1st row (wrong side): K1, p8, k1.

2nd row: P1, yb, sl 1, k1, psso, k4, inc in next st, k1, p1.

3rd to 9th rows: Rep the last 2 rows 3 times more then the first row again.

10th row: P1, C8F, p1.

11th row: As 1st row.

12th row: P1, inc in next st, k5, k2tog, p1.

13th to 19th rows: Rep the last 2 rows 3 times more then the first row again.

20th row: P1, C8B, p1.

Rep these 20 rows.

Triple Criss Cross Cable

Worked over 26 sts on a background of reverse St st.

1st row (right side): P5, [C4F, p2] twice, C4F, p5.

2nd row: K5, [p4, k2] twice, p4, k5.

3rd row: P4, [T3B, T3F] 3 times, p4.

4th row: K4, p2, [k2, p4] twice, k2, p2, k4.

5th row: P3, T3B, [p2, C4B] twice, p2, T3F, p3.

6th row: K3, p2, k3, p4, k2, p4, k3, p2, k3.

7th row: P2, T3B, p2, [T3B, T3F] twice, p2, T3F, p2.

8th row: K2, p2, k3, p2, k2, p4, k2, p2, k3, p2, k2.

9th row: P1, [T3B, p2] twice, C4F, [p2, T3F] twice, p1.

10th row: K1, [p2, k3] twice, p4, [k3, p2] twice, k1.

11th row: [T3B, p2] twice, T3B, [T3F, p2] twice, T3F.

12th row: [P2, k3] twice, p2, k2, [p2, k3] twice, p2.

13th row: [K2, p3] twice, k2, p2, [k2, p3] twice, k2.

14th row: As 12th row.

15th row: [T3F, p2] twice, T3F, [T3B, p2] twice, T3B.

16th row: As 10th row.

17th row: P1, [T3F, p2] twice, C4F, [p2, T3B] twice, p1.

18th row: As 8th row.

19th row: [P2, T3F] twice, T3B, T3F, [T3B, p2] twice.

20th row: As 6th row.

21st row: P3, T3F, [p2, C4B] twice, p2, T3B, p3.

22nd row: As 4th row.

23rd row: P4, [T3F, T3B] 3 times, p4.

24th row: As 2nd row.

Rep these 24 rows.

Cable with Bobbles

Panel of 9 sts on a background of reverse St st.

1st row (right side): P2, T5R, p2.

2nd row: K2, p2, k1, p2, k2.

3rd row: P1, T3B, p1, T3F, p1.

4th row: K1, p2, k3, p2, k1.

5th row: T3B, p3, T3F.

6th row: P2, k5, p2.

7th row: K2, p2, MB, p2, k2.

8th row: As 6th row.

9th row: T3F, p3, T3B.

10th row: As 4th row.

11th row: P1, T3F, p1, T3B, p1.

12th row: As 2nd row.

Rep these 12 rows.

Textured Cable 1

Panel of 13 sts on a background of reverse St st.

1st row (right side): P3, C3B, p1, C3F, p3.

2nd row: K3, p3, k1, p3, k3.

3rd row: P2, C3B, p1, k1, p1, C3F, p2.

4th row: K2, p3, k1, p1, k1, p3, k2.

5th row: P1, C3B, p1, [k1, p1] twice, C3F, p1.

6th row: K1, p3, k1, [p1, k1] twice, p3, k1.

7th row: C3B, p1, [k1, p1] 3 times, C3F.

8th row: P3, k1, [p1, k1] 3 times, p3.

9th row: K2, p1, [k1, p1] 4 times, k2.

10th row: P2, k1, [p1, k1] 4 times, p2.

11th row: T3F, p1, [k1, p1] 3 times, T3B.

12th row: K1, p2, k1, [p1, k1] 3 times, p2, k1.

13th row: P1, T3F, p1, [k1, p1] twice, T3B, p1.

14th row: K2, p2, k1, [p1, k1] twice, p2, k2.

15th row: P2, T3F, p1, k1, p1, T3B, p2.

16th row: K3, p2, k1, p1, k1, p2, k3.

17th row: P3, T3F, p1, T3B, p3.

18th row: K4, p2, k1, p2, k4.

19th row: P4, C5B, p4.

20th row: K4, p5, k4.

Rep these 20 rows.

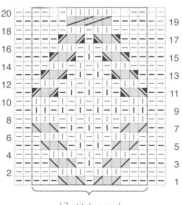

13-stitch panel

Crossroads Cable

Panel of 12 sts on a background of reverse St st.

1st row (right side): P3, T3B, T3F, p3.

2nd row: K3, p2, k2, p2, k3.

3rd row: P2, T3B, p2, T3F, p2.

4th row: K2, p2, k4, p2, k2.

5th row: P1, T3B, p4, T3F, p1.

6th row: K1, p2, k6, p2, k1.

7th row: T3B, p6, T3F.

8th row: P2, k8, p2.

9th row: T3F, p6, T3B.

10th row: As 6th row.

11th row: P1, T3F, p4, T3B, p1.

12th row: As 4th row.

13th row: P2, T3F, p2, T3B, p2.

14th row: As 2nd row.

15th row: P3, T3F, T3B, p3.

16th row: K4, p4, k4.

17th row: P4, C4B, p4.

18th row: K4, p4, k4.

Rep these 18 rows.

12-stitch panel

Pillar Cable

Panel of 5 sts on a background of reverse St st.

1st row (right side): K1, [C2F] twice.

2nd row: P1, [C2BW] twice.

Rep these 2 rows.

5-stitch panel

Use markers to denote the beginning/end of pattern repeats (or even every 20 stitches or so if a single repeat contains a lot of stitches).

Horn Cable

Panel of 16 sts on a background of reverse St st.

1st row (right side): K4, C4B, C4F, k4.

2nd row: P16.

3rd row: K2, C4B, k4, C4F, k2.

4th row: P16.

5th row: C4B, k8, C4F.

6th row: P16.

Rep these 6 rows.

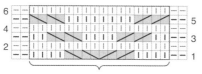

16-stitch panel

Framed Cross Cable

Panel of 16 sts on a background of reverse St st.

1st row (right side): K2, p3, T3B, T3F, p3, k2.

2nd row: P2, k3, p2, k2, p2, k3, p2.

3rd row: K2, p2, T3B, p2, T3F, p2, k2.

4th row: P2, k2, p2, k4, p2, k2, p2.

5th row: K2, p1, T3B, p4, T3F, p1, k2.

6th row: P2, k1, p2, k6, p2, k1, p2.

7th row: K2, T3B, p6, T3F, k2.

8th row: P4, k8, p4.

9th row: C4F, p8, C4B.

10th row: As 8th row.

11th row: K2, T3F, p6, T3B, k2.

12th row: As 6th row.

13th row: K2, p1, T3F, p4, T3B, p1, k2.

14th row: As 4th row.

15th row: K2, p2, T3F, p2, T3B, p2, k2.

16th row: As 2nd row.

17th row: K2, p3, T3F, T3B, p3, k2.

18th row: P2, k4, p4, k4, p2.

19th row: K2, p4, C4B, p4, k2.

20th row: As 18th row.

Rep these 20 rows.

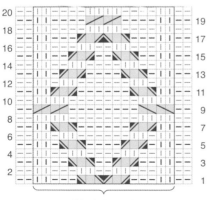

16-stitch panel

Open and Closed Cable 1

Panel of 8 sts on a background of reverse St st.

Special Abbreviations

T6F rib (Twist 6 Front rib) = slip next 3 sts onto cable needle and hold at front of work, k1, p1, k1 from left-hand needle, then k1, p1, k1 from cable needle.

T4R rib (Twist 4 Right rib) = slip next st onto cable needle and hold at back of work, k1, p1, k1 from left-hand needle, then p1 from cable needle.

T4L rib (Twist 4 Left rib) = slip next 3 sts onto cable needle and hold at front of work, p1 from left-hand needle, then k1, p1, k1 from cable needle.

1st row (right side): P1, k1, p1, k2, p1, k1, p1.

2nd row: K1, p1, k1, p2, k1, p1, k1.

3rd row: P1, T6F rib, p1.

4th row: As 2nd row.

5th row: T4R rib, T4L rib.

6th row: P1, k1, p1, k2, p1, k1, p1.

7th row: K1, p1, k1, p2, k1, p1, k1.

8th to 12th rows: Rep the last 2 rows twice more, then 6th row again.

13th row: T4L rib, T4R rib.

14th to 16th rows: As 2nd to 4th rows.

17th and 18th rows: As 1st and 2nd rows.

Rep these 18 rows.

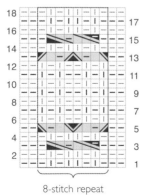

8-stitch repeat

Slipped 3-Stitch Cable

Panel of 3 sts on a background of reverse St st.

Slipped to the left:

1st row (right side): Sl 1 purlwise, k2.

2nd row: P2, sl 1 purlwise.

3rd row: C3L.

4th row: Purl.

Rep these 4 rows.

Slipped to the right:

1st row (right side): K2, sl 1 purlwise.

2nd row: Sl1 purlwise, p2.

3rd row: C3R.

4th row: Purl.

Rep these 4 rows.

Four Section Cable

Panel of 7 sts on a background of reverse St st.

Special Abbreviation

T7B rib (Twist 7 Back rib) = slip next 4 sts onto cable needle and hold at back of work, k1, p1, k1 from left-hand needle, then [p1, k1] twice from cable needle.

1st row (right side): K1, [p1, k1] 3 times.

2nd row: PB1, [k1, PB1] 3 times.

3rd row: T7B rib.

4th row: As 2nd row.

5th to 10th rows: Rep 1st and 2nd rows 3 times.

Rep these 10 rows.

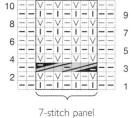

7-stitch panel

Smocking Stitch Pattern

Multiple of 8 + 7.

1st row (right side): P1, k1, *p3, k1; rep from * to last st, p1.

2nd row: K1, p1, *k3, p1; rep from * to last st, k1.

3rd row (smocking row): P1, slip next 5 sts onto cable needle and hold at front of work, wind yarn twice around sts on cable needle in a counterclockwise direction then work the stitches from the cable needle as follows: k1, p3, k1 (this will now be called 'smock 5'), *p3, 'smock 5'; rep from * to last st, p1.

4th to 8th rows: Rep 2nd row, then 1st and 2nd rows twice more.

9th row: P1, k1, p3, *'smock 5', p3; rep from * to last 2 sts, k1, p1.

10th row: As 2nd row.

11th and 12th rows: As 1st and 2nd rows.

Repeat these 12 rows.

Note: This method creates a small gap in the work at either side of the smocked stitches. The technique can be adapted to any rib pattern, provided the stitches on the cable needle begin and end with a knit stitch. The number of rows between the smocked stitches can also be varied as required.

Fuchsia Stitch

Multiple of 6.

Note: Sts should only be counted after the 11th and 12th rows.

1st row (right side): P2, *k2, yfrn, p4; rep from * to last 4 sts, k2, yfrn, p2.

2nd row: K2, *p3, k4; rep from * to last 5 sts, p3, k2.

3rd row: P2, *k3, yfrn, p4; rep from * to last 5 sts, k3, yfrn, p2.

4th row: K2, *p4, k4; rep from * to last 6 sts, p4, k2.

5th row: P2, *k4, yfrn, p4; rep from * to last 6 sts, k4, yfrn, p2.

6th row: K2, *p5, k4; rep from * to last 7 sts, p5, k2.

7th row:: P2, *k3, k2tog, p4; rep from * to last 7 sts, k3, k2tog, p2.

8th row: As 4th row.

9th row: P2, *k2, k2tog, p4; rep from * to last 6 sts, k2, k2tog, p2.

10th row: As 2nd row.

11th row: P2, *k1, k2tog, p4; rep from * to last 5 sts, k1, k2tog, p2.

12th row: K2, *p2, k4; rep from * to last 4 sts, p2, k2.

Rep these 12 rows.

Defined Diamonds

Multiple of 8 + 10.

1st row (right side): P3, C4B, *p4, C4B; rep from * to last 3 sts, p3.

2nd row: K3, p4, *k4, p4; rep from * to last 3 sts, k3.

3rd row: P1, *T4B, T4F; rep from * to last st, p1.

4th row: K1, p2, k4, *p4, k4; rep from * to last 3 sts, p2, k1.

5th row: P1, k2, p4, *C4B, p4; rep from * to last 3 sts, k2, p1.

6th row: As 4th row.

7th row: P1, *T4F, T4B; rep from * to last st, p1.

8th row: As 2nd row.

Rep these 8 rows.

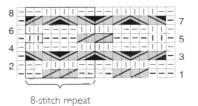

8-stitch repeat

Woven Cable Stitch I

Multiple of 4.

1st row (right side): *C4F; rep from * to end.

2nd row: Purl.

3rd row: K2, *C4B; rep from * to last 2 sts, k2.

4th row: Purl.

Rep these 4 rows.

The crochet hook makes binding off faster, easier, and much neater, and doesn't stretch any stitches. It can be used on any pattern stitch, including ribbing.

Cable with Stripes

Multiple of 13 + 1.

1st row (right side): P1, [k1, p1] twice, T2B, T2F, *p1, [k1, p1] 4 times, T2B, T2F; rep from * to last 5 sts, p1, [k1, p1] twice.

2nd row: [K1, p1] 3 times, k2, *p1, [k1, p1] 5 times, k2; rep from * to last 6 sts, [p1, k1] 3 times.

3rd row: P1, [k1, p1] twice, T2F, T2B, *p1, [k1, p1] 4 times, T2F, T2B; rep from * to last 5 sts, p1, [k1, p1] twice.

4th row: [K1, p1] twice, k2, p2, k2, *p1, [k1, p1] 3 times, k2, p2, k2; rep from * to last 4 sts, [p1, k1] twice.

5th row: [P1, k1] twice, p2, C2B, p2, *k1, [p1, k1] 3 times, p2, C2B, p2; rep from * to last 4 sts, [k1, p1] twice.

6th row: As 4th row.

Rep these 6 rows.

13-stitch repeat

Medallion Moss Cable

Panel of 13 sts on a background of reverse St st..

1st row (right side): K4, [p1, k1] 3 times, k3.

2nd row: P3, [k1, p1] 4 times, p2.

3rd and 4th rows: Rep 1st and 2nd rows once more.

5th row: C6F, k1, C6B.

6th row: Purl.

7th row: Knit.

8th to 11th rows: Rep last 2 rows.

12th row: Purl.

13th row: C6B, k1, C6F.

14th row: As 2nd row.

15th row: As 1st row.

16th row: As 2nd row.

Rep these 16 rows.

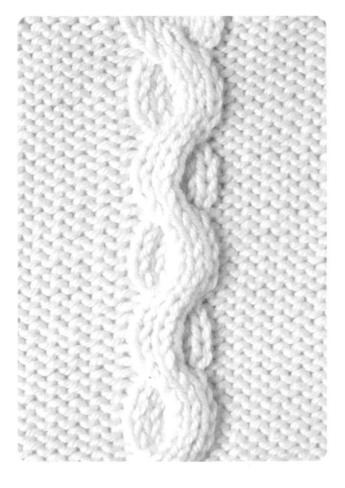

Bold Cable

Panel of 6 sts on a background of reverse St st.

1st row (right side): K6.

2nd row: P6.

3rd row: C6B.

4th row: P6.

5th to 8th rows: Rep 1st and 2nd rows twice.

9th row: C6F.

10th row: P6.

11th and 12th rows: As 1st and 2nd rows.

Rep these 12 rows.

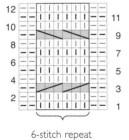

6-stitch repeat

Wandering Cable

Panel of 12 sts on a background of reverse St st.

Note: Increases to be made by purling into front and back of next st.

1st row (wrong side): K2, p4, k6.

2nd row: P6, k4, p2.

3rd row: As 1st row.

4th row: P6, C4F, p2.

5th row: As 1st row.

6th row: P4, p2tog, k4, inc in next st, p1.

7th row: K3, p4, k5.

8th row: P5, C4F, p3.

9th row: As 7th row.

10th row: P3, p2tog, k4, inc in next st, p2.

11th row: K4, p4, k4.

12th row: P4, C4F, p4.

13th row: As 11th row.

14th row: P2, p2tog, k4, inc in next st, p3.

15th row: K5, p4, k3.

16th row: P3, C4F, p5.

17th row: As 15th row.

18th row: P1, p2tog, k4, inc in next st, p4.

19th row: K6, p4, k2.

20th row: P2, C4F, p6.

21st row: As 19th row.

22nd row: P2, k4, p6.

23rd row: As 19th row.

24th row: P2, C4B, p6.

25th row: As 19th row.

26th row: P1, inc in next st, k4, p2tog, p4.

27th row: As 15th row.

28th row: P3, C4B, p5.

29th row: As 15th row.

30th row: P2, inc in next st, k4, p2tog, p3.

31st row: As 11th row.

32nd row: P4, C4B, p4.

33rd row: As 11th row.

34th row: P3, inc in next st, k4, p2tog, p2.

35th row: As 7th row.

36th row: P5, C4B, p3.

37th row: As 7th row.

38th row: P4, inc in next st, k4, p2tog, p1.

39th row: As 1st row.

40th row: P6, C4B, p2.

Rep these 40 rows.

Crossed Cable with Pincers

Panel of 18 sts on a background of reverse St st.

1st row (right side): P1, T3B, p1, k2, p4, k2, p1, T3F, p1.

2nd row: K1, p2, k2, p2, k4, p2, k2, p2, k1.

3rd row: P1, k2, p2, T3F, p2, T3B, p2, k2, p1.

4th row: K1, p2, k3, p2, k2, p2, k3, p2, k1.

5th row: T2B, T2F, p2, T3F, T3B, p2, T2B, T2F.

6th row: P1, k2, p1, k3, p4, k3, p1, k2, p1.

7th row: K1, p2, k1, p3, C4F, p3, k1, p2, k1.

8th row: As 6th row.

9th row: T2F, p1, k1, p2, T3B, T3F, p2, k1, p1, T2B.

10th row: [K1, p1] twice, k2, [p2, k2] twice, [p1, k1] twice.

11th row: P1, T2F, k1, p1, T3B, p2, T3F, p1, k1, T2B, p1.

12th row: K5, p2, k4, p2, k5.

13th row: P4, T3B, p4, T3F, p4.

14th row: K4, p2, k6, p2, k4.

15th row: P3, T3B, p6, T3F, p3.

16th row: K3, p2, k8, p2, k3.

17th row: P2, T3B, p8, T3F, p2.

18th row: K2, p2, k10, p2, k2.

Rep these 18 rows.

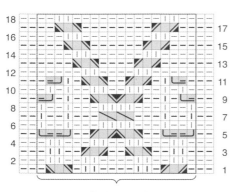

18-stitch panel

2nd row: K3, p2, k1, p1, k1, p2,

3rd row: P2, T3B, k1, p1, k1, T3F, p2.

4th row: K2, p2, [k1, p1] twice, k1, p2, k2.

5th row: P1, T3B, [k1, p1] twice, k1, T3F, p1.

6th row: K1, p2, [k1, p1] 3 times, k1, p2, k1.

7th row: T3B, [k1, p1] 3 times, k1, T3F.

8th row: P2, [k1, p1] 4 times, k1, p2.

9th row: K3, [p1, k1] 3 times, p1, k3.

10th row: P3, [k1, p1] 3 times, k1, p3.

11th row: T3F, [k1, p1] 3 times, k1, T3B.

12th row: K1, p3, [k1, p1] twice, k1, p3, k1.

13th row: P1, T3F, [k1, p1] twice, k1, T3B, p1.

14th row: K2, p3, k1, p1, k1, p3, k2.

15th row: P2, T3F, k1, p1, k1, T3B, p2.

16th row: K3, p3, k1, p3, k3.

17th row: P3, T3F, k1, T3B, p3.

18th row: K4, p5, k4.

19th row: P4, T5R, p4.

20th row: K4, p2, k1, p1, k4.

21st row: P3, T3B, p1, T3F, p3.

22nd row: [K3, p2] twice, k3.

23rd row: [P3, k2] twice, p3.

24th row: As 22nd row.

25th row: P3, T3F, p1, T3B, p3.

26th row: As 20th row.

27th row: As 19th row.

28th row: As 20th row.

Rep these 28 rows.

Cabled Moss Stitch 1

Worked over 13 sts on a background of reversed St st.

1st row (right side): P3, T3B, k1, T3F, p3.

2nd row: K3, p2, k1, p1, k1, p2, k3.

Stems with Leaves Cable

Multiple of 12 + 3.

1st row (right side): K3, *p2, T2B, k1, T2F, p2, k3; rep from * to end.

2nd row: P3, *k2, p1, [k1, p1] twice, k2, p3; rep from * to end.

3rd row: K3, *p1, T2B, p1, k1, p1, T2F, p1, k3; rep from * to end.

4th row: P3, *k1, p1, [k2, p1] twice, k1, p3; rep from * to end.

5th row: K3, *T2B, p2, k1, p2, T2F, k3; rep from * to end.

6th row: P3, *k4, p1, k4, p3; rep from * to end.

Rep these 6 rows.

12-stitch repeat

Climbing Cable

Panel of 4 sts on a background of reverse St st.

1st row (right side): K4.

2nd row: P4.

3rd row: C4B.

4th row: P4.

5th to 8th rows: Rep 1st to 4th rows once more.

9th to 12th rows: Rep 1st and 2nd rows twice.

Rep these 12 rows.

4-stitch panel

Alternated Cable

Worked over 10 sts on a background of reverse St st.

1st row (right side): P1, k8, p1.

2nd row: K1, p8, k1.

3rd row: P1, C4B, C4F, p1.

4th row: K1, p2, k4, p2, k1.

5th row: T3B, p4, T3F.

6th row: P2, k6, p2.

7th row: K2, p6, k2.

8th to 10th rows: Rep 6th and 7th rows once more, then 6th row again.

11th row: T3F, p4, T3B.

12th row: As 4th row.

13th row: P1, C4F, C4B, p1.

14th row: K1, p8, k1.

15th row: P1, C4B, C4F, p1.

16th row: K1, p8, k1.

17th row: P1, k8, p1.

18th to 20th rows: Rep 14th, 15th, and 16th rows once more.

Rep these 20 rows.

6-Stitch Spiral Cable

Panel of 6 sts on a background of reverse St st.

1st row (right side): [C2F] 3 times.

2nd row: Purl.

3rd row: K1, [C2F] twice, k1.

4th row: Purl.

Rep these 4 rows.

.

Slipped Double Chain

Worked over 7 sts.

1st row (right side): Sl 1 purlwise, k5, sl 1 purlwise.

2nd row: Sl 1 purlwise, p5, sl 1 purlwise.

3rd row: C3L, k1, C3R.

4th row: Purl.

5th row: K2, sl 1 purlwise, k1, sl 1 purlwise, k2.

6th row: P2, sl 1 purlwise, p1, sl 1 purlwise, p2.

7th row: C3R, k1, C3L.

8th row: Purl.

Rep these 8 rows.

Honeycomb Pattern

Worked over a multiple of 8 sts. The example shown is worked over 24 sts.

1st row (right side): *C4B, C4F; rep from * to end of panel.

2nd row: Purl.

3rd row: Knit.

4th row: Purl.

5th row: *C4F, C4B; rep from * to end of panel.

6th row: Purl.

7th row: Knit.

8th row: Purl.

Rep these 8 rows.

Chunky Cable

Panel of 10 sts on a background of reverse St st.

1st row (right side): K10.

2nd row: P10.

3rd row: C10F.

4th row: P10.

5th to 10th rows: Rep 1st and 2nd rows 3 times.

Rep these 10 rows.

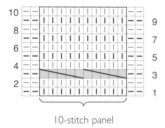

10-stitch panel

Small Moss Stitch Cable

Panel of 5 sts on a background of reverse St st.

1st row (wrong side): [P1, k1] twice, p1.

2nd row: K2, p1, k2.

3rd to 5th rows: Rep 1st and 2nd rows once more, then the 1st row again.

6th row: Slip next st onto cable needle and hold at front of work, slip next 3 sts onto 2nd cable needle and hold at back of work, knit next st from left-hand needle, knit the 3 sts from 2nd cable needle, then knit st from 1st cable needle.

7th to 11th rows: Work 5 rows in St st, starting purl.

12th row: As 6th row.

13th to 16th rows: Work 1st and 2nd rows twice more.

Rep these 16 rows.

Roman Cable

Panel of 4 sts on a background of reverse St st.

1st row (right side): C2B, C2F.

2nd row: P4.

Rep these 2 rows.

4-stitch repeat

Tulip Cable 1

Panel of 12 sts on a background of reverse St st.

1st row (right side): K12.

2nd row: P12.

3rd row: C12B.

4th row: P12.

5th to 12th rows: Rep 1st and 2nd rows 4 times.

Rep these 12 rows.

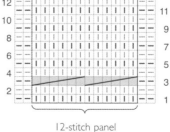

12-stitch panel

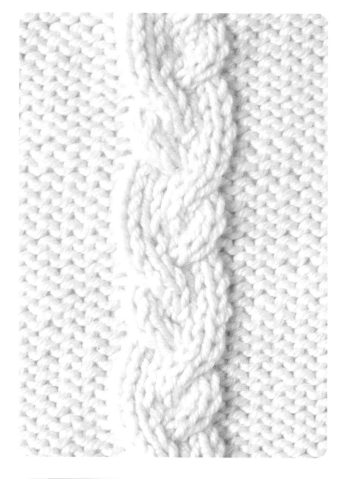

Garden Path Cable

Panel of 6 sts on a background of reverse St st.

1st row (right side): K2, C4F.

2nd row: P6.

3rd row: K6.

4th row: P6.

5th and 6th rows: As 1st and 2nd rows.

7th row: C4B, k2.

8th row: P6.

9th and 10th rows: As 3rd and 4th rows.

11th and 12th rows: As 7th and 8th rows.

Rep these 12 rows.

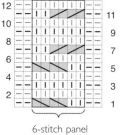

6-stitch panel

Country Lane Cable

Panel of 10 sts on a background of reverse St st.

1st row (right side): K10.

2nd row: P10.

3rd row: C10F.

4th row: P10.

5th to 12th rows: Rep 1st and 2nd rows 4 times.

13th row: C10B.

14th row: P10.

15th to 20th rows: Rep 1st and 2nd rows 3 times.

Rep these 20 rows.

10-stitch panel

Cabled Moss Stitch II

Panel of 13 sts on a background of reverse St st.

1st row (right side): P3, T3B, k1, T3F, p3.

2nd row: K3, p2, k1, p1, k1, p2, k3.

3rd row: P2, T3B, k1, p1, k1, T3F, p2.

4th row: K2, p2, [k1, p1] twice, k1, p2, k2.

5th row: P1, T3B, [k1, p1] twice, k1, T3F, p1.

6th row: K1, p2, [k1, p1] 3 times, k1, p2, k1.

7th row: T3B, [k1, p1] 3 times, k1, T3F.

8th row: P2, [k1, p1] 4 times, k1, p2.

9th row: K3, [p1, k1] 3 times, p1, k3.

10th row: P3, [k1, p1] 3 times, k1, p3.

11th row: T3F, [k1, p1] 3 times, k1, T3B.

12th row: K1, p3, [k1, p1] twice, k1, p3, k1.

13th row: P1, T3F, [k1, p1] twice, k1, T3B, p1.

14th row: K2, p3, k1, p1, k1, p3, k2.

15th row: P2, T3F, k1, p1, k1, T3B, p2.

16th row: K3, p3, k1, p3, k3.

17th row: P3, T3F, k1, T3B, p3.

18th row: K4, p5, k4.

19th row: P4, T5R, p4.

20th row: K4, p2, k1, p2, k4.

21st row: P3, T3B, p1, T3F, p3.

22nd row: [K3, p2] twice, k3.

23rd row: [P3, k2] twice, p3.

24th row: As 22nd row.

25th row: P3, T3F, p1, T3B, p3.

26th row: As 20th row.

27th row: As 19th row.

28th row: As 20th row.

Rep these 28 rows.

Stacked Cable

Panel of 8 sts on a background of reverse St st.

1st row (right side): K8.

2nd row: P8.

3rd row: C4B, C4F.

4th row: P8.

Rep these 4 rows.

8-stitch panel

Why not frame your gauge check swatches? Cast on an additional 8 stitches on your swatch, keeping 4 stitches at the beginning and end of each row in garter stitch. This will give a border to the swatch and prevent it from rolling—and it makes measuring a lot easier.

5th row: P3, T3B, p6, T3F, p3.

6th row: K3, p2, k8, p2, k3.

7th row: P2, T3B, p8, T3F, p2.

8th row: K2, p2, k10, p2, k2.

9th row: P1, T3B, p10, T3F, p1.

10th row: K1, p2, k12, p2, k1.

11th row: T3B, p12, T3F.

12th row: P2, k14, p2.

13th row: K2, p14, k2.

14th to 16th rows: Rep 12th and 13th rows once more, then 12th row again.

17th row: T3F, p12, T3B.

18th row: As 10th row.

19th row: P1, T3F, p10, T3B, p1.

20th row: As 8th row.

21st row: P2, T3F, p8, T3B, p2.

22nd row: As 6th row.

23rd row: P3, T3F, p6, T3B, p3.

24th row: As 4th row.

25th row: P4, T3F, p4, T3B, p4.

26th row: As 2nd row.

27th row: P5, C4F, C4B, p5.

28th row: K5, p8, k5.

29th row: P5, C4B, C4F, p5.

30th row: As 28th row.

31st row: P5, k8, p5.

32nd to 39th rows: Rep the last 4 rows twice more.

40th row: As 28th row.

Rep these 40 rows.

Open and Closed Cable II

Panel of 18 sts on a background of reverse St st.

1st row (right side): P5, C4B, C4F, p5.

2nd row: K5, p2, k4, p2, k5.

3rd row: P4, T3B, p4, T3F, p4.

4th row: K4, p2, k6, p2, k4.

Twisted Eyelet Cable

Panel of 8 sts on a background of reverse St st.

1st row (right side): Knit.

2nd row and every alt row: Purl.

3rd row: K2, yf, slip next 2 sts onto cable needle and hold at front of work, k2tog from left-hand needle, then k2tog from cable needle, yf, k2.

5th row: Knit.

7th row: C3F, k2, C3B.

9th row: K1, C3F, C3B, k1.

10th row: Purl

Rep these 10 rows.

Cable and Dot

Panel of 15 sts on a background of reverse St st.

1st row (wrong side): K2, k into front, back, front, back and front of next st (bobble made), k2, p2, k1, p2, k2, make bobble in next st as before, k2.

2nd row: P2, k5tog tbl (completing bobble), p2, C5F, p2, k5tog tbl, p2.

3rd row: K5, p2, k1, p2, k5.

4th row: P4, T3B, p1, T3F, p4.

5th row: K4, p2, k3, p2, k4.

6th row: P3, T3B, p3, T3F, p3.

7th row: K3, p2, k2, make bobble in next st (as on 1st row), k2, p2, k3.

8th row: P2, T3B, p2, k5tog tbl, p2, T3F, p2.

9th row: K2, p2, k7, p2, k2.

10th row: P1, T3B, p7, T3F, p1.

11th row: K1, p2, k2, make bobble in next st, k3, make bobble in next st, k2, p2, k1.

12th row: T3B, p2, k5tog tbl, p3, k5tog tbl, p2, T3F.

13th row: P2, k11, p2.

14th row: K2, p11, k2.

15th row: P2, k3, make bobble in next st, k3, make bobble in next st, k3, p2.

16th row: T3F, p2, k5tog tbl, p3, k5tog tbl, p2, T3B.

17th row: K1, p2, k9, p2, k1.

18th row: P1, T3F, p7, T3B, p1.

19th row: K2, p2, k3, make bobble in next st, k3, p2, k2.

20th row: P2, T3F, p2, k5tog tbl, p2, T3B, p2.

21st row: K3, p2, k5, p2, k3.

22nd row: P3, T3F, p3, T3B, p3.

23rd row: K4, p2, k3, p2, k4.

24th row: P4, T3F, p1, T3B, p4.

Rep these 24 rows.

Note: The cable as given here twists to the left. To work the cable twisted to the right, work C5B instead of C5F on the 2nd row.

Cable with Horn Detail

Panel of 6 sts on a background of reverse St st.

1st row (right side): K1, C2B, C2F, k1.

2nd row: P6.

3rd row: C2B, k2, C2F.

4th row: P6.

Rep these 4 rows.

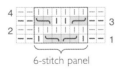

6-stitch panel

Large Woven Cable

Panel of 20 sts on a background of reverse St st.

1st row (right side): K20.

2nd row: P20.

3rd row: K4, [C8F] twice.

4th row: P20.

5th to 8th rows: Rep 1st and 2nd rows twice.

9th row: [C8B] twice, k4.

10th row: P20.

11th and 12th rows: As 1st and 2nd rows.

Rep these 12 rows.

20-stitch panel

last 3 sts, p3.

16th row: K3, p1, *k4, p1; rep from * to last 3 sts, k3.

17th row: P2, *T2B, p4, T2F, p2; rep from * to end.

18th row: K2, *p1, k6, p1, k2; rep from * to end.

19th row: P2, k1, p6, *T2F, T2B, p6; rep from * to last 3 sts, k1, p2.

20th row: K2, p1, k7, C2BW, *k8, C2BW; rep from * to last 10 sts, k7, p1, k2.

21st row: P2, k1, p6, *T2B, T2F, p6; rep from * to last 3 sts, k1, p2.

22nd to 29th rows: Rep the last 4 rows twice more.

30th row: As 18th row.

31st row: P2, *T2F, p1, T2B, p2; rep from * to end.

32nd row: As 16th row.

Rep these 32 rows.

Rocket Cable

Multiple of 10 + 12.

1st row (right side): P3, T2F, p2, T2B, *p4, T2F, p2, T2B; rep from * to last 3 sts, p3.

2nd row: K4, p1, k2, p1, *k6, p1, k2, p1; rep from * to last 4 sts, k4.

3rd row: P4, T2F, T2B, *p6, T2F, T2B; rep from * to last 4 sts, p4.

4th row: K5, C2BW, *k8, C2BW; rep from * to last 5 sts, k5.

5th row: P4, T2B, T2F, *p6, T2B, T2F; rep from * to last 4 sts, p4.

6th to 13th rows: Rep the last 4 rows twice more.

14th row: As 2nd row.

15th row: P3, T2B, p2, T2F, *p4, T2B, p2, T2F; rep from * to

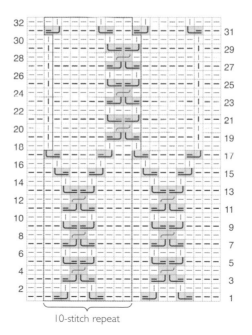

10-stitch repeat

Tight Braid Cable

Panel of 10 sts on a background of reverse St st.

1st row (wrong side): Purl.

2nd row: K2, [C4F] twice.

3rd row: Purl.

4th row: [C4B] twice, k2.

Rep these 4 rows.

Free Cable

Panel of 7 sts on a background of reverse St st.

1st row (right side): [T2F] twice, p3.

2nd row: K3, [PB1, k1] twice.

3rd row: P1, [T2F] twice, p2.

4th row: K2, PB1, k1, PB1, k2.

5th row: P2, [T2F] twice, p1.

6th row: [K1, PB1] twice, k3.

7th row: P3, [T2F] twice.

8th row: PB1, k1, PB1, k4.

9th row: P4, k1, p1, k1.

10th row: As 8th row.

11th row: P3, [T2B] twice.

12th row: As 6th row.

13th row: P2, [T2B] twice, p1.

14th row: As 4th row.

15th row: P1, [T2B] twice, p2.

16th row: As 2nd row.

17th row: [T2B] twice, p3.

18th row: K4, PB1, k1, PB1.

19th row: K1, p1, k1, p4.

20th row: As 18th row.

Rep these 20 rows.

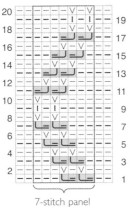

7-stitch panel

Raised Circle Cable

Panel of 4 sts on a background of reverse St st.

1st row (right side): C2B, C2F.

2nd row: P4.

3rd row: C2F, C2B.

4th row: P4.

Rep these 4 rows.

4-stitch panel

Small Raised Circle Cable

Panel of 4 sts on a background of reverse St st.

1st row (right side): C2B, C2F.

2nd row: P4.

3rd and 4th rows: Rep the last 2 rows once more.

5th row: C2F, C2B.

6th row: P4.

7th and 8th rows: Rep the last 2 rows once more.

Rep these 8 rows.

4-stitch panel

Folded Cable 1

Panel of 10 sts on a background of reverse St st.

1st row (right side): K10.

2nd row: P10.

3rd row: C10B.

4th row: P10.

5th to 8th rows: Rep 1st and 2nd rows twice.

9th row: K2, C6B, k2.

10th row: P10.

11th to 14th rows: Rep 1st and 2nd rows twice.

15th and 16th rows: As 9th and 10th rows.

17th and 18th rows: As 1st and 2nd rows.

Rep these 18 rows.

Linking Ovals

Panel of 8 sts on a background of reverse St st.

1st row (right side): P2, C4B, p2.

2nd row: K2, p4, k2.

3rd row: P1, T3B, T3F, p1.

4th row: K1, p2, k2, p2, k1.

5th row: T3B, p2, T3F.

6th row: P2, k4, p2.

7th row: K2, p4, k2.

8th row: P2, k4, p2.

9th row: T3F, p2, T3B.

10th row: K1, p2, k2, p2, k1.

11th row: P1, T3F, T3B, p1.

12th row: K2, p4, k2.

Rep these 12 rows.

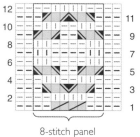

8-stitch panel

Propellor Cable

Panel of 6 sts on a background of reverse St st.

1st row (right side): K6.

2nd row: P6.

3rd row: C6F.

4th row: P6.

5th to 10th rows: Rep 1st and 2nd rows once, then rep 1st to 4th rows once.

11th to 20th rows: rep 1st and 2nd rows 5 times.

Rep these 20 rows.

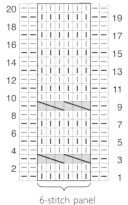

6-stitch panel

Lace Cable Pattern

Panel of 8 sts on a background of reverse St st.

1st row (right side): K2, yo, sl 1, k1, psso, k4.

2nd and every alt row: Purl.

3rd row: K3, yo, sl 1, k1, psso, k3.

5th row: K4, yo, sl 1, k1, psso, k2.

7th row: K5, yo, sl 1, k1, psso, k1.

9th row: C6B, yo, sl 1, k1, psso.

10th row: Purl.

Rep these 10 rows.

Cable with Braid

Panel of 6 sts on a background of reverse St st.

1st row (right side): K2, C4F.

2nd row: P6.

3rd row: C4B, k2.

4th row: P6.

Rep these 4 rows.

6-stitch panel

The cable needle should be about the same size or smaller than the working needles; certainly not larger, as this would be difficult to knit from after the stitches are crossed.

Cable Fabric

Multiple of 6.

1st row: Knit.

2nd and every alt row: Purl.

3rd row: *K2, C4B; rep from * to end.

5th row: Knit.

7th row: *C4F, k2; rep from * to end.

8th row: Purl.

Rep these 8 rows.

Sweeping Cable

Panel of 8 sts on a background of reverse St st.

1st row (right side): K8.

2nd row: P8.

3rd row: C8B.

4th row: P8.

5th to 8th rows: Rep 1st and 2nd rows twice.

Rep these 8 rows.

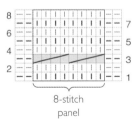

8-stitch panel

Vine Cable

Panel of 9 sts on a background of reverse St st.

1st row (right side): K9.

2nd row: P9.

3rd row: K3, C6F.

4th row: P9.

5th to 10th rows: Rep 1st and 2nd rows twice, then rep 3rd and 4th rows once.

11th and 12th rows: As 1st and 2nd rows.

13th row: C6B, k3.

14th row: P9.

15th to 18th rows: Rep 1st and 2nd rows twice.

19th and 20th rows: As 13th and 14th rows.

Rep these 20 rows.

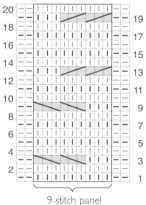

9-stitch panel

Filled Diamond Cable

Panel of 12 sts on a background of reverse St st.

1st row (right side): P2, k8, p2.

2nd row: K2, p8, k2.

3rd row: P3, C3B, T3F, p3.

4th row: K3, p3, k1, p2, k3.

5th row: P2, T3B, k1, p1, C3F, p2.

6th row: K2, p2, k1, p1, k1, p3, k2.

7th row: P1, C3B, [p1, k1] twice, T3F, p1.

8th row: K1, p3, k1, [p1, k1] twice, p2, k1.

9th row: T3B, [k1, p1] 3 times, C3F.

10th row: P2, k1, [p1, k1] 3 times, p3.

11th row: T3F, [k1, p1] 3 times, T3B.

12th row: As 8th row.

13th row: P1, T3F, [p1, k1] twice, T3B, p1.

14th row: As 6th row.

15th row: P2, T3F, k1, p1, T3B, p2.

16th row: As 4th row.

17th row: P3, T3F, T3B, p3.

18th row: K4, p4, k4.

19th row: P2, C4B, C4F, p2.

20th row: K2, p8, k2.

21st and 22nd rows: As 1st and 2nd rows.

23rd and 24th rows: As 19th and 20th rows.

Rep these 24 rows.

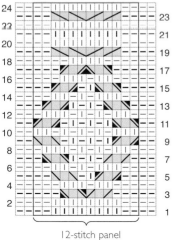

12-stitch panel

Open Cable

Panel of 7 sts on a background of reverse St st.

1st row (right side): K7.

2nd row: P7.

3rd row: C3R, k1, C3L.

4th row: P7.

Rep these 4 rows.

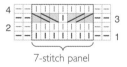

7-stitch panel

Medium Circle Cable

Panel of 8 sts on a background of reverse St st.

1st row (right side): K8.

2nd and every alt row: P8.

3rd row: C4B, C4F.

5th row: K8.

7th row: C4F, C4B.

8th row: P8.

Rep these 8 rows.

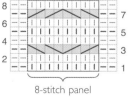

8-stitch panel

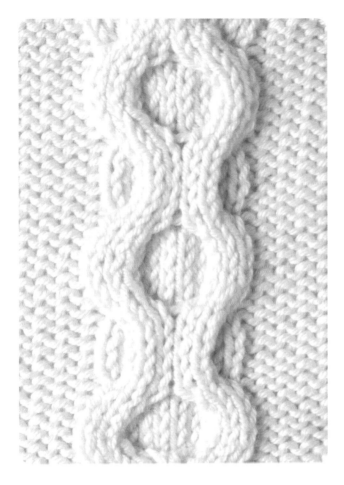

Large Circle Cable

Panel of 12 sts on a background of reverse St st.

1st row (right side): K12.

2nd row: P12.

3rd row: C6B, C6F.

4th row: P12.

5th to 8th rows: Rep 1st and 2nd rows twice.

9th row: C6F, C6B.

10th row: P12.

11th and 12th rows: As 1st and 2nd rows.

Rep these 12 rows.

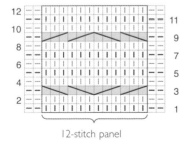

12-stitch panel

Divided Cable I

Panel of 12 sts on a background of reverse St st.

1st row (right side): [K1, p1] 4 times, T4B.

2nd row: K1, p3, [k1, p1] 4 times.

3rd row: [K1, p1] 3 times, T4B, T2F.

4th row: P1, k2, p3, [k1, p1] 3 times.

5th row: [K1, p1] twice, T4B, T2F, T2B.

6th row: K1, C2BW, k2, p3, [k1, p1] twice.

7th row: K1, p1, T4B, T2F, T2B, T2F.

8th row: P1, k2, C2FW, k2, p3, k1, p1.

9th row: T4B, [T2F, T2B] twice.

10th row: K1, C2BW, k2, C2BW, k3, p2.

11th row: T4FP, [T2B, T2F] twice.

12th row: As 8th row.

13th row: K1, p1, T4FP, T2B, T2F, T2B.

14th row: As 6th row.

15th row: [K1, p1] twice, T4FP, T2B, T2F.

16th row: As 4th row.

17th row: [K1, p1] 3 times, T4FP, T2B.

18th row: As 2nd row.

19th row: [K1, p1] 4 times, T4FP.

20th row: P2, [k1, p1] 5 times.

Rep these 20 rows.

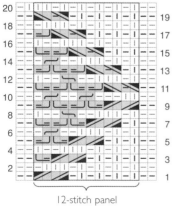

12-stitch panel

Disappearing Cable

Panel of 18 sts on a background of reverse St st.

1st row (right side): P6, k6, p6.

2nd row: K6, p6, k6.

3rd row: P3, k3, C6F, k3, p3.

4th row: K3, p12, k3.

5th row: P3, k12, p3.

6th to 8th rows: Rep 4th and 5th rows once more, then 4th row again.

9th row: K3, T6B, T6F, k3.

10th row: P6, k6, p6.

11th row: K6, p6, k6.

12th to 14th rows: Rep 10th and 11th rows once more then 10th row again.

15th row: T6B, p6, T6F.

16th row: P3, k12, p3.

17th row: K3, p12, k3.

18th to 20th rows: Rep 16th and 17th rows once more then 16th row again.

21st row: C6F, p6, C6B.

22nd to 26th rows: Rep 10th and 11th rows twice then 10th row again.

27th row: P3, C6F, C6B, p3.

28th to 32nd rows: Work 4th and 5th rows twice then 4th row again.

33rd row: P6, C6F, p6.

34th row: As 2nd row.

35th row: As 1st row.

36th row: As 2nd row.

Rep these 36 rows.

Overlapping Cable

Panel of 6 sts on a background of reverse St st.

1st row (right side): K6.

2nd row: P6.

3rd row: C6B.

4th row: P6.

5th and 6th rows: As 1st and 2nd rows.

7th row: K1, C4B, k1.

8th row: P6.

9th to 12th rows: Rep the last 4 rows once more.

Rep these 12 rows.

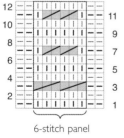

6-stitch panel

Checkered Cable

Panel with a multiple of 4 + 2.

Example shown is worked over 10 sts on a background of reverse St st.

1st row (right side): K2, *C4F; rep from * to end.

2nd row: Purl.

3rd row: *C4B; rep from * to last 2 sts, k2.

4th row: Purl.

Rep these 4 rows.

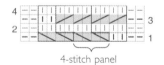

4-stitch panel

Divided Cable II

Panel of 12 sts on a background of reverse St st.

1st row (right side): T4F, [p1, k1] 4 times.

2nd row: [P1, k1] 4 times, p3, k1.

3rd row: T2B, T4F, [p1, k1] 3 times.

4th row: [P1, k1] 3 times, p3, k2, p1.

5th row: T2F, T2B, T4F, [p1, k1] twice.

6th row: [P1, k1] twice, p3, k2, C2FW, k1.

7th row: T2B, T2F, T2B, T4F, p1, k1.

8th row: P1, k1, p3, k2, C2BW, k2, p1.

9th row: [T2F, T2B] twice, T4F.

10th row: P2, k3, C2FW, k2, C2FW, k1.

11th row: [T2B, T2F] twice, T4BP.

12th row: As 8th row.

13th row: T2F, T2B, T2F, T4BP, p1, k1.

14th row: As 6th row.

15th row: T2B, T2F, T4BP, [p1, k1] twice.

16th row: As 4th row.

17th row: T2F, T4BP, [p1, k1] 3 times.

18th row: As 2nd row.

19th row: T4BP, [p1, k1] 4 times.

20th row: [P1, k1] 5 times, p2.

Rep these 20 rows.

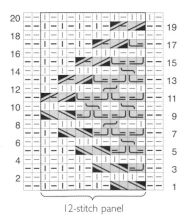

12-stitch panel

Bulky Cable

Panel of 6 sts on a background of reverse St st.

1st row (right side): K6.

2nd row: P6.

3rd row: C6B.

4th row: P6

Rep these 4 rows.

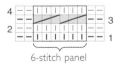

12–Stitch Braid

Panel of 12 sts on a background of reverse St st.

1st row (right side): K12.

2nd row: P12.

3rd row: K4, C8B.

4th row: P12.

5th and 6th rows: As 1st and 2nd rows.

7th row: C8F, k4.

8th row: P12.

Rep these 8 rows.

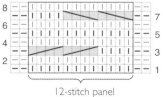

Raised Curve Cable

Panel of 4 sts on a background of reverse St st.

1st row (right side): K4.

2nd row and every alt row: P4.

3rd row: C4B.

5th row: K4.

7th row: C4F.

8th row: P4.

Rep these 8 rows.

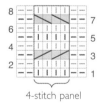

4-stitch panel

Filled Oval Cable

Panel of 8 sts on a background of reverse St st.

1st row (right side): K8.

2nd row: P8.

3rd row: C8B.

4th row: P8.

5th and 6th rows: As 1st and 2nd rows.

7th row: K2, C4B, k2.

8th row: P8.

9th to 12th rows: Rep the last 4 rows once more.

Rep these 12 rows.

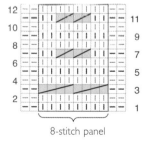

8-stitch panel

Bell Cable

Worked over 26 sts on a background of reverse St st.

1st row (right side): K2, [p3, k2] twice, p2, [k2, p3] twice, k2.

2nd row: P2, [k3, p2] twice, k2, p2, [k3, p2] twice.

3rd to 10th rows: Rep 1st and 2nd rows 4 times more.

11th row: T5L, k2, T5R, p2, T5L, k2, T5R.

12th row: K3, p6, k8, p6, k3.

13th row: P3, k6, p8, k6, p3.

14th to 18th rows: Rep 12th and 13th rows twice more, then the 12th row again.

19th row: P3, C6F, p8, C6B, p3.

20th row: K3, p6, k8, p6, k3.

Rep these 20 rows.

Sprinkle a small amount of baby powder on your hands before knitting to help draw the yarn smoothly through your fingers.

Touching Paths

Panel of 9 sts on a background of reverse St st.

1st row (right side): P3, T4B, k2.

2nd row: P2, k2, p2, k3.

3rd row: P1, T4B, p1, T3B.

4th row: K1, p2, k3, p2, k1.

5th row: T3B, p1, T4B, p1.

6th row: K3, p2, k2, p2.

7th row: K2, T4B, p3.

8th row: K5, p4.

9th row: C4B, p5.

10th row: K5, p4.

11th row: K2, T4F, p3.

12th row: As 6th row.

13th row: T3F, p1, T4F, p1.

14th row: As 4th row.

15th row: P1, T4F, p1, T3F.

16th row: As 2nd row.

17th row: P3, T4F, k2.

18th row: P4, k5.

19th row: P5, C4B.

20th row: P4, k5.

Rep these 20 rows.

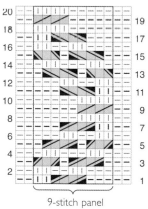

9-stitch panel

Roman Pillar II

Panel of 16 sts on a background of reverse St st.

1st row (right side): P4, C4R, T4L, p4.

2nd row: K4, p3, k1, p4, k4.

3rd row: P3, C4R, p1, k1, T4L, p3.

4th row: K3, p3, k1, p1, k1, p4, k3.

5th row: P2, C4R, [p1, k1] twice, T4L, p2.

6th row: K2, p3, k1, [p1, k1] twice, p4, k2.

7th row: P1, C4R, [p1, k1] 3 times, T4L, p1.

8th row: K1, p3, k1, [p1, k1] 3 times, p4, k1.

9th row: C4R, [p1, k1] 4 times, T4L.

10th row: P3, k1, [p1, k1] 4 times, p4.

11th row: T4L, [k1, p1] 4 times, T4R.

12th row: As 8th row.

13th row: P1, T4L, [k1, p1] 3 times, T4R, p1.

14th row: As 6th row.

15th row: P2, T4L, [k1, p1] twice, T4R, p2.

16th row: As 4th row.

17th row: P3, T4L, k1, p1, T4R, p3.

18th row: As 2nd row.

19th row: P4, T4L, T4R, p4.

20th row: K5, p6, k5.

21st row: P5, C6B, p5.

22nd row: K5, p6, k5.

Rep these 22 rows.

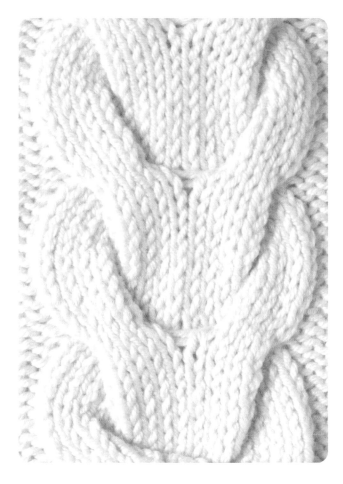

Trophy Cable 1

Panel of 20 sts on a background of reverse St st.

1st row (right side): K20.

2nd row: P20.

3rd row: C10B, C10F.

4th row: P20.

5th to 12th rows: Rep 1st and 2nd rows 4 times.

Rep these 12 rows.

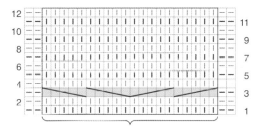

20-stitch panel

Gauge samples should never be measured while on the needle because the needle distorts the fabric.

Double Diamonds

Panel of 20 sts on a background of reverse St st.

1st row (right side): P6, T4BP, T4FP, p6.

2nd row: K6, [p2, k1] twice, p2, k6.

3rd row: P4, T4B, p1, k2, p1, T4F, p4.

4th row: K4, [p2, k3] twice, p2, k4.

5th row: P2, T4B, p2, C2B, C2F, p2, T4F, p2.

6th row: K2, p2, k4, p4, k4, p2, k2.

7th row: T4B, p2, C4B, C4F, p2, T4F.

8th row: P2, k4, p8, k4, p2.

9th row: T4F, C4B, k4, C4F, T4B.

10th row: K2, p16, k2.

11th row: P2, C4B, k8, C4F, p2.

12th row: K2, p16, k2.

13th row: T4B, T4F, k4, T4B, T4F.

14th row: As 8th row.

15th row: T4F, p2, T4F, T4B, p2, T4B.

16th row: As 6th row.

17th row: P2, T4F, p2, T2F, T2B, p2, T4B, p2.

18th row: As 4th row.

19th row: P4, T4F, p1, k2, p1, T4B, p4.

20th row: As 2nd row.

21st row: P6, T4F, T4B, p6.

22nd row: K8, p4, k8.

23rd row: P8, k4, p8.

24th row: K8, p4, k8.

Rep these 24 rows.

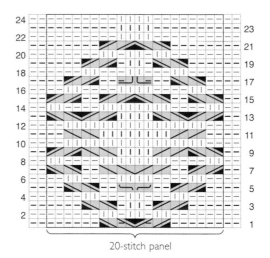

20-stitch panel

Moss Stitch Hearts

Worked over 19 sts.

1st row (right side): P6, T3B, k1, T3F, p6.

2nd row: K6, p3, k1, p3, k6.

3rd row: P5, C3B, p1, k1, p1, C3F, p5.

4th row: K5, p2, [k1, p1] twice, k1, p2, k5.

5th row: P4, T3B, [k1, p1] twice, k1, T3F, p4.

6th row: K4, p3, [k1, p1] twice, k1, p3, k4.

7th row: P3, C3B, [p1, k1] 3 times, p1, C3F, p3.

8th row: K3, p2, [k1, p1] 4 times, k1, p2, k3.

9th row: P2, T3B, [k1, p1] 4 times, k1, T3F, p2.

10th row: K2, p3, [k1, p1] 4 times, k1, p3, k2.

11th row: P1, C3B, [p1, k1] 5 times, p1, C3F, p1.

12th row: K1, p2, [k1, p1] 6 times, k1, p2, k1.

13th row: T3B, [k1, p1] 6 times, k1, T3F.

14th row: P3, [k1, p1] 6 times, k1, p3.

15th row: K2, [p1, k1] 7 times, p1, k2.

16th row: As 14th row.

17th row: T4F, [p1, k1] 5 times, p1, T4B.

18th row: K2, p3, [k1, p1] 4 times, k1, p3, k2.

19th row: P2, T4F, [p1, k1] 3 times, p1, T4B, p2.

20th row: K7, p2, k1, p2, k7.

Rep these 20 rows.

Bobbles may be knitted into this pattern by working the 19th row as follows:- P2, T4F, p1, k1, p1, MB, p1, k1, p1, T4B, p2.

Interlocking Cable

Panel of 12 sts on a background of reverse St st.

1st row (right side): K12.

2nd row: P12.

3rd row: C6B, C6F.

4th row: P12.

5th to 8th rows: Rep 1st and 2nd rows twice.

9th and 10th rows: As 3rd and 4th rows.

11th to 14th rows: Rep 1st and 2nd rows twice.

15th row: C6F, C6B.

16th row: P12.

17th and 20th rows: Rep 1st and 2nd rows twice.

21st and 22nd rows: As 15th and 16th rows.

23rd and 24th rows: As 1st and 2nd rows.

Rep these 24 rows.

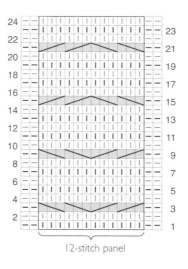

12-stitch panel

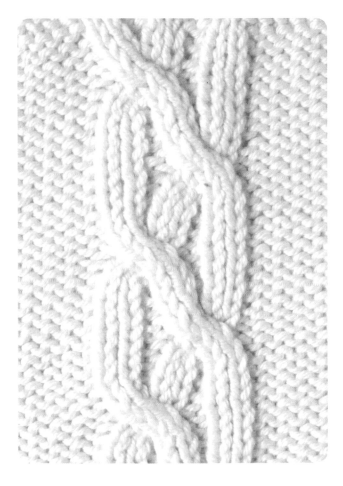

Crossing Paths

Panel of 10 sts on a background of reverse St st.

Special Abbreviation

T6L rib (Twist 6 Left rib) = slip next 4 sts onto cable needle and hold at front of work, knit next 2 sts from left-hand needle, slip the 2 purl sts from cable needle back to left-hand needle and purl them, then knit 2 sts from cable needle.

1st row (right side): K2, [p2, k2] twice.

2nd row: P2, [k2, p2] twice.

3rd row: T6L rib, p2, k2.

4th row: As 2nd row.

5th to 8th rows: Rep 1st and 2nd rows twice.

9th row: K2, p2, T6L rib.

10th row: As 2nd row.

11th and 12th rows: As 1st and 2nd rows.

Rep these 12 rows.

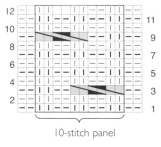

10-stitch panel

Lattice Pattern I

Multiple of 4 + 6.

1st row (right side): P1, *T2F, T2B; rep from * to last st, p1.

2nd row: K2, *C2BW, k2; rep from * to end.

3rd row: P1, *T2B, T2F; rep from * to last st, p1.

4th row: K1, p1, k2, *C2FW, k2; rep from * to last 2 sts, p1, k1.

Rep these 4 rows.

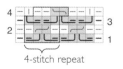

4-stitch repeat

Trophy Cable II

Panel of 16 sts on a background of reverse St st.

1st row (right side): K16.

2nd row: P16.

3rd row: C8B, C8F.

4th row: P16.

5th to 8th rows: Rep 1st and 2nd rows twice.

Rep these 8 rows.

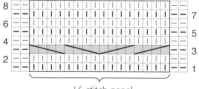

16-stitch panel

Inserted Cable

Panel of 14 sts on a background of reverse St st.

1st row (wrong side): K5, p4, k5.

2nd row: P5, C4F, p5.

3rd row: K5, p4, k5.

4th row: P4, T3B, T3F, p4.

5th row: K4, p2, k2, p2, k4.

6th row: P3, T3B, p2, T3F, p3.

7th row: K3, p2, k4, p2, k3.

8th row: P2, T3B, p4, T3F, p2.

9th row: K2, p2, k6, p2, k2.

10th row: P1, [T3B] twice, [T3F] twice, p1.

11th row: [K1, p2] twice, k2, [p2, k1] twice.

12th row: [T3B] twice, p2, [T3F] twice.

13th row: P2, k1, p2, k4, p2, k1, p2.

14th row: K1, T2F, T3F, p2, T3B, T2B, k1.

15th row: [P1, k1] twice, p2, k2, p2, [k1, p1] twice.

16th row: K1, p1, T2F, T3F, T3B, T2B, p1, k1.

17th row: P1, k2, p1, k1, p4, k1, p1, k2, p1.

18th row: T2F, T2B, p1, C4F, p1, T2F, T2B.

19th row: K1, C2B, k2, p4, k2, C2F, k1.

Rep rows 4 to 18.

Slanting Stripes

Multiple of 6 + 4.

1st row (right side): P1, *T3F, p3; rep from * to last 3 sts, p3.

2nd row: K6, p2, *k4, p2; rep from * to last 2 sts, k2.

3rd row: P2, *T3F, p3; rep from * to last 2 sts, p2.

4th row: K5, p2, *k4, p2; rep from * to last 3 sts, k3.

5th row: *P3, T3F; rep from * to last 4 sts, p4.

6th row: K4, *p2, k4; rep from * to end.

7th row: P4, *T3F, p3; rep from * to end.

8th row: K3, *p2, k4; rep from * to last st, k1.

9th row: P5, T3F, *p3, T3F; rep from * to last 2 sts, p2.

10th row: K2, *p2, k4; rep from * to last 2 sts, k2.

11th row: P6, T3F, *p3, T3F; rep from * to last st, p1.

12th row: K1, *p2, k4; rep from * to last 3 sts, k3.

Rep these 12 rows.

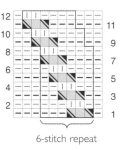

6-stitch repeat

Dancing Cable

Panel of 16 sts on a background of reverse St st.

1st row (right side): P2, C4F, p4, C4F, p2.

2nd row: K2, p4, k4, p4, k2.

3rd row: P2, k4, p4, k4, p2.

4th row: As 2nd row.

5th and 6th rows: As 1st and 2nd rows.

7th row: [T4B, T4F] twice.

8th row: P2, k4, p4, k4, p2.

9th row: K2, p4, C4F, p4, k2.

10th row: As 8th row.

11th row: K2, p4, k4, p4, k2.

12th row: As 8th row.

13th to 22nd rows: rep the last 4 rows twice more, then 9th and 10th rows again.

23rd row: [T4F, T4B] twice.

24th row: As 2nd row.

Rep these 24 rows.

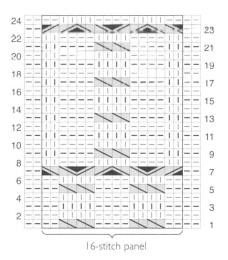

16-stitch panel

Open Bobble Pattern

Multiple of 4 + 2.

1st row (right side): Purl

2nd row: K1, *M3, k3tog; rep from * to last st, k1.

3rd row: Purl.

4th row: K1, *k3tog, M3; rep from * to last st, k1.

Rep these 4 rows.

4-stitch panel

Chunky Braid

Panel with a multiple of 6 + 9.

Example shown is worked over 15 sts on a background of reverse St st.

1st row (right side): Knit.

2nd row: Purl.

3rd row: K3, *C6F; rep from * to end.

4th row: Purl.

5th and 6th rows: As 1st and 2nd rows.

7th row: *C6B; rep from * to last 3 sts, k3.

8th row: Purl.

Rep these 8 rows.

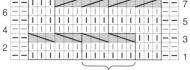

6-stitch repeat

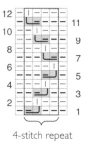

Zig-Zag Cable 1

Multiple of 4 + 2.

1st row (right side): P3, T2B, *p2, T2B; rep from * to last st, p1.

2nd row: K2, *p1, k3; rep from * to end.

3rd row: P2, *T2B, p2; rep from * to end.

4th row: *K3, p1; rep from * to last 2 sts, k2.

5th row: P1, T2B, *p2, T2B; rep from * to last 3 sts, p3.

6th row: K4, p1, *k3, p1; rep from * to last st, k1.

7th row: P1, T2F, *p2, T2F; rep from * to last 3 sts, p3.

8th row: As 4th row.

9th row: P2, *T2F, p2; rep from * to end.

10th row: As 2nd row.

11th row: P3, T2F, *p2, T2F; rep from * to last st, p1.

12th row: K1, p1, *k3, p1; rep from * to last 4 sts, k4.

Rep these 12 rows.

Note: This stitch is also very effective when worked as a panel of 4 sts on a background of reverse St st.

4-stitch repeat

Open V Stitch

Panel of 12 sts on a background of reverse St st.

1st row (right side): P3, C3B, C3F, p3.

2nd row: K3, p6, k3.

3rd row: P2, C3B, k2, C3F, p2.

4th row: K2, p8, k2.

5th row: P1, T3B, k4, T3F, p1.

6th row: K1, p2, k1, p4, k1, p2, k1.

7th row: T3B, p1, C4B, p1, T3F.

8th row: P2, k2, p4, k2, p2.

Rep these 8 rows.

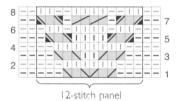

12-stitch panel

Cable with Swirl

Panel of 22 sts on a background of reverse St st.

Special Abbreviations

Work 5tog (Work 5 sts together) = with yarn at back of work, slip 3 sts purlwise, *pass 2nd st on right-hand needle over 1st (center) st, slip center st back to left-hand needle, pass 2nd st on left-hand needle over*, slip center st back to right-hand needle; rep from * to * once more, purl center st. (Note: Stitch referred to as 'center st' is center one of 5 sts).

1st row (right side): T4B, p1, T4F, T4B, p9.

2nd row: K11, p4, k5, p2.

3rd row: K2, p5, C4B, p11.

4th row: As 2nd row.

5th row: T4F, p1, T4B, T4F, p9.

6th row: K9, p2, k4, p2, k1, p2, k2.

7th row: P2, work 5tog, p4, T4F, p4, M5K, p2.

8th row: K2, p2, k1, p2, k4, p2, k9.

9th row: P9, T4F, T4B, p1, T4F.

10th row: P2, k5, p1, k11.

11th row: P11, C4F, p5, k2.

12th row: As 10th row.

13th row: P9, T4B, T4F, p1, T4B.

14th row: As 8th row.

15th row: P2, M5K, p4, T4B, p4, work 5tog, p2.

16th row: As 6th row.

Rep these 16 rows.

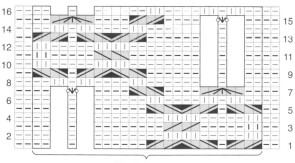

22-stitch panel

Bobble with Cable

Panel of 9 sts on a background of reverse St st.

Special Abbreviation

MB#4 (Make Bobble number 4) = (K1, p1) twice all into next st (turn and p4, turn and k4) twice, turn and p4, turn and sl 2, k2tog, p2sso (bobble completed).

1st row (right side): P1, T3B, p1, T3F, p1.

2nd row: K1, p2, k3, p2, k1.

3rd row: T3B, p3, T3F.

4th row: P2, k5, p2.

5th row: K2, p2, MB#4, p2, k2.

6th row: P2, k5, p2.

7th row: T3F, p3, T3B.

8th row: As 2nd row.

9th row: P1, T3F, p1, T3B, p1.

10th row: K2, p5, k2.

11th row: P2, T5BP, p2.

12th row: K2, p5, k2.

Rep these 12 rows.

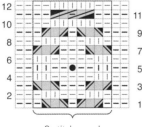

9-stitch panel

Little Cable Fabric

Multiple of 4 + 1.

1st row (right side): K1, *sl 1 purlwise, k3; rep from * to end.

2nd row: *P3, sl 1 purlwise; rep from * to last st, p1.

3rd row: K1, *C3L, k1; rep from * to end.

4th row: Purl.

5th row: K5, *sl 1, k3; rep from * to end.

6th row: *P3, sl 1; rep from * to last 5 sts, p5.

7th row: K3, *C3R, k1; rep from * to last 2 sts, k2.

8th row: Purl.

Rep these 8 rows.

Loose V Stitch

Panel of 12 sts on a background of reverse St st.

1st row (right side): P3, T3B, T3F, p3.

2nd row: K3, p2, k2, p2, k3.

3rd row: P2, T3B, p2, T3F, p2.

4th row: K2, p2, k4, p2, k2.

5th row: P1, T3B, p4, T3F, p1.

6th row: K1, p2, k6, p2, k1.

7th row: T3B, p6, T3F.

8th row: P2, k8, p2.

Rep these 8 rows.

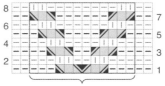

12-stitch panel

Woven Cable

Worked over a multiple of 8 + 4 sts on a background of reverse St st (minimum 20 sts). The example shown is worked over 28 sts.

1st row (right side): Knit.

2nd row and every alt row: K2, purl to 2 sts before end of panel, k2.

3rd row: Knit.

5th row: K2, *C8B; rep from * to 2 sts before end of panel, k2.

7th row: Knit.

9th row: Knit.

11th row: K6, *C8F; rep from * to 6 sts before end of panel, k6.

12th row: As 2nd row.

Rep these 12 rows.

Rippled Diamonds

Panel of 11 sts on a background of reverse St st.

Special Abbreviation

T3RP (Twist 3 Right Purl) = slip next 2 sts onto cable needle and hold at back of work, knit next st from left-hand needle, then p1, k1 from cable needle.

1st row (right side): P3, T2B, k1, T2F, p3.

2nd row: K3, p1, [k1, p1] twice, k3.

3rd row: P2, T2B, k1, p1, k1, T2F, p2.

4th row: K2, p1, [k1, p1] 3 times, k2.

5th row: P1, T2B, k1, [p1, k1] twice, T2F, p1.

6th row: K1, [p1, k1] 5 times.

7th row: T2B, k1, [p1, k1] 3 times, T2F.

8th row: P1, [k1, p1] 5 times.

9th row: T2F, p1, [k1, p1] 3 times, T2B.

10th row: As 6th row.

11th row: P1, T2F, p1, [k1, p1] twice, T2B, p1.

12th row: As 4th row.

13th row: P2, T2F, p1, k1, p1, T2B, p2.

14th row: As 2nd row.

15th row: P3, T2F, p1, T2B, p3.

16th row: K4, p1, k1, p1, k4.

17th row: P4, T3RP, p4.

18th row: As 16th row.

Rep these 18 rows.

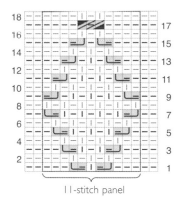

11-stitch panel

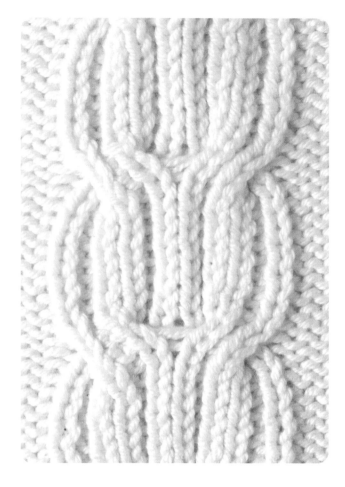

Cable with Segments

Panel of 16 sts on a background of reverse St st.

Special Abbreviations

T8B rib (Twist 8 Back rib) = slip next 4 sts onto cable needle and hold at back of work, k1, p2, k1 from left-hand needle, then k1, p2, k1 from cable needle.

T8F rib (Twist 8 Front rib) = slip next 4 sts onto cable needle and hold at front of work, k1, p2, k1 from left-hand needle, then k1, p2, k1 from cable needle.

1st row (right side): K1, p2, [k2, p2] 3 times, k1.

2nd row: P1, k2, [p2, k2] 3 times, p1.

3rd row: T8B rib, T8F rib.

4th row: As 2nd row.

5th to 12th rows: Rep 1st and 2nd rows 4 times.

Rep these 12 rows.

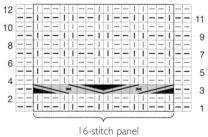

16-stitch panel

Bobbles and Waves

Worked over 26 sts on a background of reverse St st.

1st row (right side): P2, T3B, p5, C6B, p5, T3F, p2.

2nd row: K2, p2, k6, p6, k6, p2, k2.

3rd row: P1, T3B, p4, T5B, T5F, p1, T3F, p1.

4th row: K1, p2, k5, p3, k4, p3, k5, p2, k1.

5th row: T3B, p3, T5B, p4, T5F, p3, T3F.

6th row: P2, k1, make bobble as follows: knit into front, back and front of next st, [turn and knit these 3 sts] 3 times, then turn and sl 1, k2tog, psso (bobble completed), k2, p3, k8, p3, k2, make bobble as before, k1, p2.

7th row: T3F, p3, k3, p8, k3, p3, T3B.

8th row: K1, p2, k3, p3, k8, p3, k3, p2, k1.

9th row: P1, T3F, p2, T5F, p4, T5B, p2, T3B, p1.

10th row: K2, p2, [k4, p3] twice, k4, p2, k2.

11th row: P2, T3F, p3, T5F, T5B, p3, T3B, p2.

12th row: K1, make bobble as before, k1, p2, k5, p6, k5, p2, k1, make bobble, k1.

Rep these 12 rows.

To help remember which side of your work is which, try using different-colored needles of the same size—one color for right-side rows and the other for wrong-side rows.

Lattice Pattern

Worked over a multiple of 16 + 1 (minimum 33) on a background of reverse St st. The example shown is worked over 33 sts.

1st row (right side): K1, *yo, k2, sl 1, k1, psso, p7, k2tog, k2, yo, k1; rep from * to end.

2nd row: P5, *k7, p9; rep from * to last 12 sts, k7, p5.

3rd row: K2, *yo, k2, sl 1, k1, psso, p5, k2tog, k2, yo, k2tog, yo, k1; rep from * to last 15 sts, yo, k2, sl 1, k1, psso, p5, k2tog, k2, yo, k2.

4th row: P6, *k5, p11; rep from * to last 11 sts, k5, p6.

5th row: *K2tog, yo, k1, yo, k2, sl 1, k1, psso, p3, k2tog, k2, yo, k2tog, yo; rep from * to last st, k1.

6th row: P7, *k3, p13; rep from * to last 10 sts, k3, p7.

7th row: K1, *k2tog, yo, k1, yo, k2, sl 1, k1, psso, p1, k2tog, k2, yo, [k2tog, yo] twice; rep from * to last 16 sts, k2tog, yo, k1, yo, k2, sl 1, k1, psso, p1, k2tog, k2, yo, k2tog, yo, k2.

8th row: P8, *k1, p15; rep from * to last 9 sts, k1, p8.

9th row: P5, *C7B, p9; rep from * to last 12 sts, C7B, p5.

10th row: K5, *p3, k1, p3, k9; rep from * to last 12 sts, p3, k1, p3, k5.

11th row: P4, *k2tog, k2, yo, k1, yo, k2, sl 1, k1, psso, p7; rep from * to last 13 sts, k2tog, k2, yo, k1, yo, k2, sl 1, k1, psso, p4.

12th row: K4, *p9, k7; rep from * to last 13 sts, p9, k4.

13th row: P3, *k2tog, k2, yo, k2tog, yo, k1, yo, k2, sl 1, k1, psso, p5; rep from * to last 14 sts, k2tog, k2, yo, k2tog, yo, k1, yo, k2, sl 1, k1, psso, p3.

14th row: K3, *p11, k5; rep from * to last 14 sts, p11, k3.

15th row: P2, *k2tog, k2, yo, [k2tog, yo] twice, k1, yo, k2, sl 1, k1, psso, p3; rep from * to last 15 sts, k2tog, k2, yo, [k2tog, yo] twice, k1, yo, k2, sl 1, k1, psso, p2.

16th row: K2, *p13, k3; rep from * to last 15 sts, p13, k2.

17th row: P1, *k2tog, k2, yo, [k2tog, yo] 3 times, k1, yo, k2, sl 1, k1, psso, p1; rep from * to end.

18th row: K1, *p15, k1; rep from * to end.

19th row: P1, k3, *p9, C7F; rep from * to last 13 sts, p9, k3, p1.

20th row: K1, p3, *k9, p3, k1, p3; rep from * to last 13 sts, k9, p3, k1.

Rep these 20 rows.

Internal Diamonds

Panel of 14 sts on a background of reverse St st.

1st row (right side): P4, C3B, C3F, p4.

2nd row: K4, [PB1] 6 times, k4.

3rd row: P3, T3B, C2B, T3F, p3.

4th row: K3, *[PB1] twice, k1; rep from * twice more, k2.

5th row: P2, T3B, p1, C2B, p1, T3F, p2.

6th row: *K2, [PB1] twice; rep from * twice more, k2.

7th row: P1, T3B, p1, T2B, T2F, p1, T3F, p1.

8th row: K1, [PB1] twice, k2, [PB1, k2] twice, [PB1] twice, k1.

9th row: T3B, p1, T2B, p2, T2F, p1, T3F.

10th row: [PB1] twice, k2, PB1, k4, PB1, k2, [PB1] twice.

11th row: K2, p2, k1, p4, k1, p2, k2.

12th row: As 10th row.

13th row: T3F, p1, T2F, p2, T2B, p1, T3B.

14th row: As 8th row.

15th row: P1, T3F, p1, T2F, T2B, p1, T3B, p1.

16th row: As 6th row.

17th row: P2, T3F, p1, C2B, p1, T3B, p2.

18th row: As 4th row.

19th row: P3, T3F, C2B, T3B, p3.

20th row: As 2nd row.

21st row: P4, T3F, T3B, p4.

22nd row: K5, [PB1] 4 times, k5.

23rd row: P5, C4B, p5.

24th row: As 22nd row.

Rep these 24 rows.

Forked Cable

Multiple of 8 + 2.

1st row (wrong side): Purl.

2nd row: P3, k4, *p4, k4; rep from * to last 3 sts, p3.

Rep the last 2 rows twice more then the 1st row again.

8th row: K3, p4, *k4, p4; rep from * to last 3 sts, k3.

9th row: Purl.

10th row: K1, *C4F, C4B; rep from * to last st, k1.

Rep these 10 rows.

Fluffy yarns such as mohair or angora can be made easier to use—just put the yarn in your freezer for an hour or so before knitting with it.

Criss-Cross Cable with Twists

Panel of 16 sts on a background of reverse St st.

1st row (right side): P2, C4F, p4, C4F, p2.

2nd row: K2, p4, k4, p4, k2.

3rd row: P2, k4, p4, k4, p2.

4th row: As 2nd row.

5th row: As 1st row.

6th row: As 2nd row.

7th row: [T4B, T4F] twice.

8th row: As 3rd row.

9th row: K2, p4, C4F, p4, k2.

10th row: As 3rd row.

11th row: As 2nd row.

12th row: As 3rd row.

13th row: As 9th row.

14th to 21st rows: Rep the last 4 rows twice more.

22nd row: As 3rd row.

23rd row: [T4F, T4B] twice.

24th row: As 2nd row.

Rep these 24 rows.

Vine and Twist

Worked over 17 sts on a background of reverse St st.

1st row (right side): P6, C5, p6.

2nd row: K6, p5, k6.

3rd row: P5, T3B, k1, T3F, p5.

4th row: K5, p2, k1, p1, k1, p2, k5.

5th row: P4, T3B, p1, k1, p1, T3F, p4.

6th row: K4, p2, k2, p1, k2, p2, k4.

7th row: P3, k2tog, k1, p2, yon, k1, yfrn, p2, k1, sl 1, k1, psso, p3.

8th row: K3, p2, k2, p3, k2, p2, k3.

9th row: P2, k2tog, k1, p2, [k1, yo] twice, k1, p2, k1, sl 1, k1, psso, p2.

10th row: K2, p2, k2, p5, k2, p2, k2.

11th row: P1, k2tog, k1, p2, k2, yo, k1, yo, k2, p2, k1, sl 1, k1, psso, p1.

12th row: K1, p2, k2, p7, k2, p2, k1.

13th row: Purl into front and back of next st (called inc 1), k2, p2, k2, insert needle into next 2 sts on left-hand needle as if to k2tog, then slip both sts onto right-hand needle without knitting them (called sl 2tog knitwise), k1, pass 2 slipped sts over (called p2sso), k2, p2, k2, inc 1.

14th row: As 10th row.

15th row: P1, inc 1, k2, p2, k1, sl 2tog knitwise, k1, p2sso, k1, p2, k2, inc 1, p1.

16th row: As 8th row.

17th row: P2, inc 1, k2, p2, sl 2tog knitwise, k1, p2sso, p2, k2, inc 1, p2.

18th row: As 6th row.

19th row: P4, T3F, p1, k1, p1, T3B, p4.

20th row: As 4th row.

21st row: P5, T3F, k1, T3B, p5.

22nd row: As 2nd row.

23rd row: As 1st row.

24th row: As 2nd row.

25th row: P6, k5, p6.

26th row: As 2nd row.

Rep these 26 rows.

Double Spiral Cable

Panel of 22 sts worked on a background of reverse St st. The number of sts within the panel varies.

Special Abbreviations

Work 5tog (Work 5 sts together) = with yarn at back of work, slip 3 sts purlwise, *pass 2nd st on right-hand needle over 1st (center) st, slip center st back to left-hand needle, pass 2nd st on left-hand needle over*, slip center st back to right-hand needle; rep from * to * once more, purl center st. (Note: Stitch referred to as 'center st' is center 1 of 5 sts).

1st row (right side). P9, k4, p9.

2nd row: K9, p4, k9.

3rd row: P9, C4B, p9.

4th row: K9, p4, k9.

5th row: P2, M5K, p4, T4B, T4F, p4, M5K, p2.

6th row: K2, p2, k1, [p2, k4] 3 times, p2, k1, p2, k2.

7th row: T4B, p1, T4F, T4B, p4, T4F, T4B, p1, T4F.

8th row: P2, k5, p4, k8, p4, k5, p2.

9th row: K2, p5, C4F, p8, C4B, p5, k2.

10th row: As 8th row.

11th row: T4F, p1, T4B, T4F, p4, T4B, T4F, p1, T4B.

12th row: As 6th row.

13th row: P2, work 5tog, p4, T4F, T4B, p4, work 5tog, p2.

14th to 16th rows: As 2nd to 4th rows.

Rep these 16 rows.

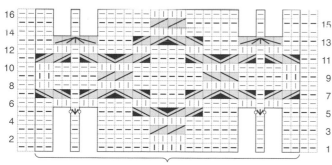

22-stitch panel

Wide Cable Panel

Panel of 20 sts on a background of reverse St st.

1st and every alt row (wrong side): Purl.

2nd row: K6, C4B, C4F, k6.

4th row: K4, C4B, k4, C4F, k4.

6th row: K2, C4B, k8, C4F, k2.

8th row: C4B, k12, C4F.

Rep these 8 rows.

Padded Cable

Panel of 20 sts on a background of reverse St st.

1st row (right side): K20.

2nd row: P20.

3rd row: C10B, C10F.

4th row: P20.

5th to 14th rows: Rep 1st and 2nd rows 5 times.

15th row: C10F, C10B.

16th row: P20.

17th to 24th rows: Rep 1st and 2nd rows 4 times.

Rep these 24 rows.

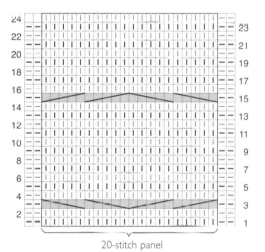

20-stitch panel

Small Wavy Cable

Multiple of 3 + 1.

1st row (right side): P1, *C2B, p1; rep from * to end.

2nd row: K1, *p2, k1; rep from * to end.

3rd row: P1, *C2F, p1; rep from * to end.

4th row: As 2nd row.

Rep these 4 rows.

3-stitch repeat

Diagonal Ripple

Multiple of 4 + 3.

1st row (right side): P4, T2B, *p2, T2B; rep from * to last st, p1.

2nd row: K2, p1, *k3, p1; rep from * to last 4 sts, k4.

3rd row: P3, *T2B, p2; rep from * to end.

4th row: K3, *p1, k3; rep from * to end.

5th row: *P2, T2B; rep from * to last 3 sts, p3.

6th row: K4, p1, *k3, p1; rep from * to last 2 sts, k2.

7th row: P1, T2B, *p2, T2B; rep from * to last 4 sts, p4.

8th row: K5, p1, *k3, p1; rep from * to last st, k1.

Rep these 8 rows.

4-stitch repeat

Diagonal Tramline Cable

Panel of 18 sts on a background of reverse St st.

1st row (right side): K2, p3, k2, p4, k2, p3, k2.

2nd row: P2, k3, p2, k4, p2, k3, p2.

3rd row: As 1st row.

4th row: As 2nd row.

5th row: [T3F, p2] twice, T3B, p2, T3B.

6th row: K1, p2, k3, p2, k2, p2, k3, p2, k1.

7th row: P1, T3F, p2, T3F, T3B, p2, T3B, p1.

8th row: K2, p2, k3, p4, k3, p2, k2.

9th row: P2, T3F, p2, C4B, p2, T3B, p2.

10th row: K3, p2, k2, p4, k2, p2, k3.

11th row: P3, [T3F, T3B] twice, p3.

12th row: K4, p4, k2, p4, k4.

13th row: P4, C4F, p2, C4F, p4.

14th row: K4, p4, k2, p4, k4.

15th row: P3, [T3B, T3F] twice, p3.

16th row: K3, p2, k2, p4, k2, p2, k3.

17th row: P2, T3B, p2, C4B, p2, T3F, p2.

18th row: K2, p2, k3, p4, k3, p2, k2.

19th row: P1, T3B, p2, T3B, T3F, p2, T3F, p1.

20th row: K1, p2, k3, p2, k2, p2, k3, p2, k1.

21st row: [T3B, p2] twice, T3F, p2, T3F.

22nd row: As 2nd row.

23rd row: As 1st row.

24th to 26th rows: Rep the last 2 rows once more then 22nd row again.

Rep these 26 rows.

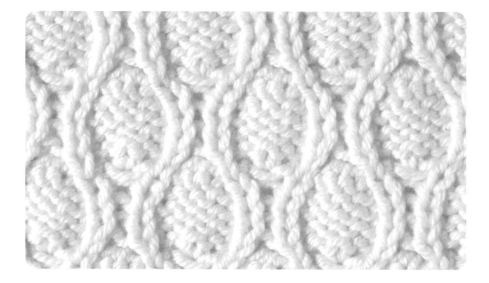

Repeated Ovals

Multiple of 8 + 1.

Special Abbreviations

Work 5tog (Work 5 sts together) = with yarn at front (wrong side), slip 3 sts purlwise, k2tog, p3sso.

1st row (right side): K1, *p5, k1, p1, k1; rep from * to end.

2nd row: P1, *k1, p1, k5, p1; rep from * to end.

3rd row: As 1st row.

4th row: P1, *M5K, p1, work 5tog, p1; rep from * to end.

5th row: K1, *p1, k1, p5, k1; rep from * to end.

6th row: P1, *k5, p1, k1, p1; rep from * to end.

7th to 9th rows: Rep 5th and 6th rows once more, then 5th row again.

10th row: P1, *work 5tog, p1, M5K, p1; rep from * to end.

11th and 12th rows: As 1st and 2nd rows.

Rep these 12 rows.

8-stitch repeat

Repeated Circles

Multiple of 6 + 2.

1st row (right side): Knit.

2nd row: Purl.

3rd row: K1, *C3R, C3L; rep from * to last st, k1.

4th row: Purl.

5th and 6th rows: As 1st and 2nd rows.

7th row: K1, *C3L, C3R; rep from * to last st, k1.

8th row: Purl.

Rep these 8 rows.

Note: This stitch is also very effective when worked as a panel with a multiple of 6 sts on a background of reverse St st.

6-stitch repeat

Small Circle Cable

Multiple of 6 + 2.

1st row (right side): P2, *C2B, C2F, p2; rep from * to end.

2nd row: K2, *p4, k2; rep from * to end.

3rd row: P2, *C2F, C2B, p2; rep from * to end.

4th row: As 2nd row.

Rep these 4 rows.

6-stitch repeat

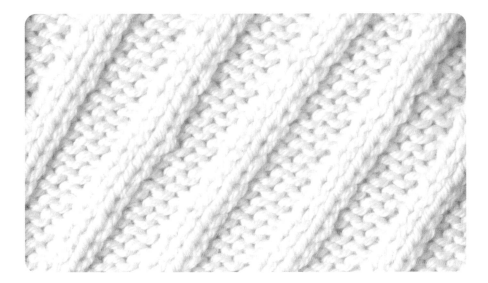

Slanting Diagonals

Multiple of 6 + 4.

1st row (right side): P6, T3B, *p3, T3B; rep from * to last st, p1.

2nd row: K2, *p2, k4; rep from * to last 2 sts, k2.

3rd row: P5, T3B, *p3, T3B; rep from * to last 2 sts, p2.

4th row: K3, *p2, k4; rep from * to last st, k1.

5th row: P4, *T3B, p3; rep from * to end.

6th row: K4, *p2, k4; rep from * to end.

7th row: *P3, T3B; rep from * to last 4 sts, p4.

8th row: K5, p2, *k4, p2; rep from * to last 3 sts, k3.

9th row: P2, *T3B, p3; rep from * to last 2 sts, p2.

10th row: K6, p2, *k4, p2; rep from * to last 2 sts, k2.

11th row: P1, *T3B, p3; rep from * to last 3 sts, p3.

12th row: K7, p2, *k4, p2; rep from * to last st, k1.

Rep these 12 rows.

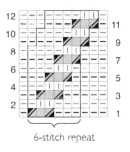

6-stitch repeat

Ornamental Cable

Panel of 30 sts on a background of reverse St st.

1st row (right side): K9, C6B, C6F, k9.

2nd row and every alt row: P30.

3rd row: K6, C6B, k6, C6F, k6.

5th row: K3, C6B, k12, C6F, k3.

7th row: C6B, k18, C6F.

8th row: P30.

Rep these 8 rows.

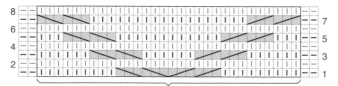

30-stitch panel

Eyelet Cable

Multiple of 8 + 1.

Special Abbreviation

C3tog (Cross 3 together) = slip next 2 sts onto cable needle and hold at back of work, knit next st from left-hand needle, then k2tog from cable needle.

1st row (right side): P1, *C3tog, p1, k3, p1; rep from * to end.

2nd row: K1, *p3, k1, p1, yrn, p1, k1; rep from * to end.

3rd row: P1, *k3, p1, C3tog, p1; rep from * to end.

4th row: K1, *p1, yrn, p1, k1, p3, k1; rep from * to end.

Rep these 4 rows.

Lace and Cables

Multiple of 11 + 7.

1st row (right side): K1, *yo, sl 1, k1, psso, k1, k2tog, yo, k6; rep from * to last 6 sts, yo, sl 1, k1, psso, k1, k2tog, yo, k1.

2nd row and every alt row: Purl.

3rd row: K2, *yo, sl 1, k2tog, psso, yo, k8; rep from * to last 5 sts, yo, sl 1, k2tog, psso, yo, k2.

5th row: As 1st row.

7th row: K2, *yo, sl 1, k2tog, psso, yo, k1, C6B, k1; rep from * to last 5 sts, yo, sl 1, k2tog, psso, yo, k2.

8th row: Purl.

Rep these 8 rows.

Remember to give your hands and wrists a break by taking 10 minutes out of your knitting session every 45 minutes or so—you'll get more knitting done in the long run.

Simple Cable

Panel of 2 sts on a background of reverse St st.

1st row (right side): C2B

2nd row: P2.

Rep these 2 rows.

2-stitch panel

Divided Bobble Cable I

Panel of 12 sts on a background of reverse St st.

1st row (right side): [K1, p1] 5 times, k2.

2nd row: P2, [k1, p1] 5 times.

3rd row: [K1, p1] 4 times, T4B.

4th row: K2, p2, [k1, p1] 4 times.

5th row: [K1, p1] 3 times, T4B, p2.

6th row: K4, p2, [k1, p1] 3 times.

7th row: [K1, p1] twice, T4B, p4.

8th row: K6, p2, [k1, p1] twice.

9th row: K1, p1, T4B, p1, MB#8, p1.

10th row: K8, p2, k1, p1.

11th row: T4B, p3, MB#8, p4.

12th row: K10, p2.

13th row: K2, p2, MB#8, p5, MB#8, p1.

14th row: K10, p2.

15th row: T4FP, p3, MB#8, p4.

16th row: As 10th row.

17th row: K1, p1, T4FP, p4, MB#8, p1.

18th row: As 8th row.

19th row: [K1, p1] twice, T4FP, p1.

20th row: As 6th row.

21st row: [K1, p1] 3 times, T4FP, p2.

22nd row: As 4th row.

23rd row: [K1, p1] 4 times, T4FP.

24th row: P2, [k1, p1] 5 times.

Rep these 24 rows.

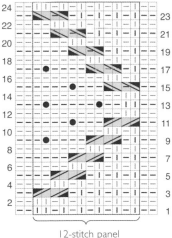

12-stitch panel

Wavy Cable Lace

Multiple of 14 + 1.

1st row (right side): K1, *yo, k2, p3, p3tog, p3, k2, yo, k1; rep from * to end.

2nd row: P4, *k7, p7; rep from * to last 11 sts, k7, p4.

3rd row: K2, *yo, k2, p2, p3tog, p2, k2, yo, k3; rep from * to last 13 sts, yo, k2, p2, p3tog, p2, k2, yo, k2.

4th row: P5, *k5, p9; rep from * to last 10 sts, k5, p5.

5th row: K3, *yo, k2, p1, p3tog, p1, k2, yo, k5; rep from * to last 12 sts, yo, k2, p1, p3tog, p1, k2, yo, k3.

6th row: P6, *k3, p11; rep from * to last 9 sts, k3, p6.

7th row: K4, *yo, k2, p3tog, k2, yo, k7; rep from * to last 11 sts, yo, k2, p3tog, k2, yo, k4.

8th row: P7, *k1, p13; rep from * to last 8 sts, k1, p7.

9th row: P2tog, *p3, k2, yo, k1, yo, k2, p3, p3tog; rep from * to last 13 sts, p3, k2, yo, k1, yo, k2, p3, p2tog.

10th row: K4, *p7, k7; rep from * to last 11 sts, p7, k4.

11th row: P2tog, *p2, k2, yo, k3, yo, k2, p2, p3tog; rep from * to last 13 sts, p2, k2, yo, k3, yo, k2, p2, p2tog.

12th row: K3, *p9, k5; rep from * to last 12 sts, p9, k3.

13th row: P2tog, *p1, k2, yo, k5, yo, k2, p1, p3tog; rep from * to last 13 sts, p1, k2, yo, k5, yo, k2, p1, p2tog.

14th row: K2, *p11, k3; rep from * to last 13 sts, p11, k2.

15th row: P2tog, *k2, yo, k7, yo, k2, p3tog; rep from * to last 13 sts, k2, yo, k7, yo, k2, p2tog.

16th row: K1, *p13, k1; rep from * to end.

Rep these 16 rows.

Crossed Cables

Multiple of 12 + 14.

1st row (right side): P3, T4B, T4F, *p4, T4B, T4F; rep from * to last 3 sts, p3.

2nd row: K3, p2, *k4, p2; rep from * to last 3 sts, k3.

3rd row: P1, *T4B, p4, T4F; rep from * to last st, p1.

4th row: K1, p2, k8, *p4, k8; rep from * to last 3 sts, p2, k1.

5th row: P1, k2, p8, *C4B, p8; rep from * to last 3 sts, k2, p1.

6th row: As 4th row.

7th row: P1, *T4F, p4, T4B; rep from * to last st, p1.

8th row: As 2nd row.

9th row: P3, T4F, T4B, *p4, T4F, T4B; rep from * to last 3 sts, p3.

10th row: K5, p4, *k8, p4; rep from * to last 5 sts, k5.

11th row: P5, C4F, *p8, C4F; rep from * to last 5 sts, p5.

12th row: As 10th row.

Rep these 12 rows.

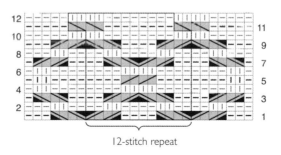

12-stitch repeat

Rose Garden

Multiple of 9 + 5.

1st row (right side): P2, KB1, p2, *k4, p2, KB1, p2; rep from * to end.

2nd row: K2, PB1, k2, *p4, k2, PB1, k2; rep from * to end.

3rd row: P2, KB1, p2, *C4B, p2, KB1, p2; rep from * to end.

4th row: As 2nd row.

Rep these 4 rows.

9-stitch repeat

Twisted and Crossed Cable

Worked over 16 sts on a background of reverse St st.

1st row (right side): P2, C4B, p4, C4F, p2.

2nd row: K2, p4, k4, p4, k2.

3rd row: P1, T3B, T3F, p2, T3B, T3F, p1.

4th row: K1, [p2, k2] 3 times, p2, k1.

5th row: [T3B, p2, T3F] twice.

6th row: P2, k4, p4, k4, p2.

7th row: K2, p4, C4B, p4, k2.

8th row: As 6th row.

9th row: K2, p4, k4, p4, k2.

10th row: As 6th row.

11th row: As 7th row.

12th row: As 6th row.

13th row: [T3F, p2, T3B] twice.

14th row: As 4th row.

15th row: P1, T3F, T3B, p2, T3F, T3B, p1.

16th row: As 2nd row.

17th row: As 1st row.

18th row: As 2nd row.

19th row: As 3rd row.

20th row: As 4th row.

21st row: P1, [k2, p2] twice, k2, slip last 6 sts worked onto cable needle and wrap yarn 4 times anti-clockwise round these 6 sts, then slip the 6 sts back onto right hand needle, p2, k2, p1.

22nd row: As 4th row.

23rd row: As 15th row.

24th row: As 2nd row.

Rep these 24 rows.

Loose Woven Cables

Multiple of 6 + 2.

1st row (right side): Knit.

2nd row: K1, knit to last st wrapping yarn twice around needle for each st, k1.

3rd row: K1, *C6B (dropping extra loops); rep from * to last st, k1.

4th and 5th rows: Work 2 rows in garter st.

6th row: K4, *knit to last 4 sts, wrapping yarn twice around needle for each st, k4.

7th row: K4, *C6F (dropping extra loops); rep from * to last 4 sts, k4.

8th row: Knit.

Rep these 8 rows.

Good posture is important when you're sitting for long periods. Sit up straight and keep your feet on the floor.

Gentle Cable

Panel of 5 sts on a background of reverse St st.

1st row (right side): C2B, k1, C2F.

2nd row: P5.

Rep these 2 rows.

5-stitch repeat

19th row: P2, *k6, p2, [k2, p2] twice, k6, p2; rep from * to end.

20th row: K2, *p6, k2, [p2, k2] twice, p6, k2; rep from * to end.

21st row: P2, *C6B, p2, [k2, p2] twice, C6F, p2; rep from * to end.

22nd row: As 20th row.

23rd and 24th rows: As 19th and 20th rows.

25th to 36th rows: Rep 19th to 24th rows twice.

Rep these 36 rows.

Lacy Leaf Trellis

Multiple of 24 + 2.

1st row (right side): P2, *k2, p2, [k6, p2] twice, k2, p2; rep from * to end.

2nd row: K2, *p2, k2, [p6, k2] twice, p2, k2; rep from * to end.

3rd row: P2, *k2, p2, C6F, p2, C6B, p2, k2, p2; rep from * to end.

4th row: As 2nd row.

5th and 6th rows: As 1st and 2nd rows.

7th to 18th rows: Rep these 6 rows twice more.

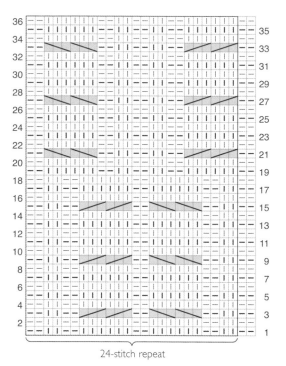

24-stitch repeat

Cupped Cable

Worked over 15 sts on a background of reverse St st.

1st row (right side): P5, T5L, p5.

2nd row: K5, p2, k1, p2, k5.

3rd row: P4, T3B, k1, T3F, p4.

4th row: K4, p2, k1, p1, k1, p2, k4.

5th row: P3, T3B, k1, p1, k1, T3F, p3.

6th row: K3, p2, [k1, p1] twice, k1, p2, k3.

7th row: P2, T3B, [k1, p1] twice, k1, T3F, p2.

8th row: K2, p2, [k1, p1] 3 times, k1, p2, k2.

9th row: P1, T3B, [k1, p1] 3 times, k1, T3F, p1.

10th row: K1, p2, [k1, p1] 4 times, k1, p2, k1.

11th row: T3B, [k1, p1] 4 times, k1, T3F.

12th row: P2, [k1, p1] 5 times, k1, p2.

Rep these 12 rows.

Twisting Cable

Panel of 3 sts on a background of reverse St st.

1st row (right side): K1, C2F.

2nd row: P1, C2BW.

Rep these 2 rows.

3-stitch panel

Wandering Paths

Multiple of 12 + 2.

Special Abbreviations

T6R rib (Twist 6 Right rib) = slip next 4 sts onto cable needle and hold at back of work, knit next 2 sts from left hand needle, slip the 2 purl sts from cable needle back to left-hand needle and purl them, then knit 2 sts from cable needle.

T6L rib (Twist 6 Left rib) = slip next 4 sts onto cable needle and hold at front of work, knit next 2 sts from left-hand needle, slip the 2 purl sts from cable needle back to left-hand needle and purl them, then knit 2 sts from cable needle.

1st row (right side): P2, *k2, p2; rep from * to end.

2nd row and every alt row: K2, *p2, k2; rep from * to end.

3rd row: P2, *T6R rib, p2, k2, p2; rep from * to end.

5th and 7th rows: As 1st row.

9th row: P2, *k2, p2, T6L rib, p2; rep from * to end.

11th row: As 1st row.

12th row: As 2nd row.

Rep these 12 rows.

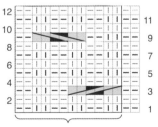

12-stitch repeat

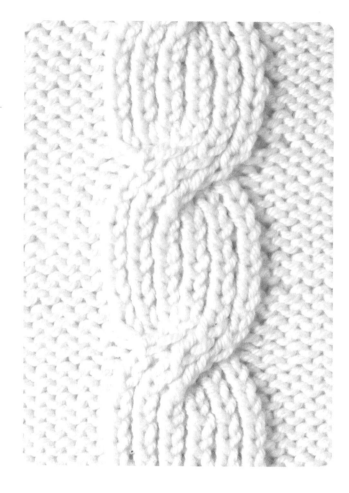

Closed Bud Cable

Panel of 11 sts on a background of reverse St st.

Special Abbreviation

T11B rib (Twist 11 Back rib) = slip next 6 sts onto cable needle and hold at back of work, k1, [p1, k1] twice from left-hand needle, then [p1, k1] 3 times from cable needle.

1st row (right side): K1, [p1, k1] 5 times.

2nd row: PB1, [k1, PB1] 5 times.

3rd row: T11B rib.

4th row: As 2nd row.

5th to 14th rows: Rep 1st and 2nd rows 5 times.

Rep these 14 rows.

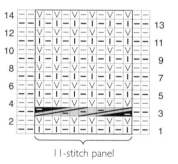

11-stitch panel

Stacked Buds

Multiple of 5 + 2.

Special Abbreviation

Bind 3 = slip 1 st purlwise with yarn at back of work, k1, yo, k1, pass slipped st over the k1, yo, k1.

1st row (right side): P2, *k3, p2; rep from * to end.

2nd row: K2, *p3, k2; rep from * to end.

3rd row: P2, *bind 3, p2; rep from * to end.

4th row: As 2nd row.

Rep these 4 rows.

5-stitch repeat

Sweeping Flowers

Multiple of 6 + 2.

1st row (right side): P2, *k4, p2; rep from * to end.

2nd row: K2, *p4, k2; rep from * to end.

3rd row: P2, *C4B, p2; rep from * to end.

4th row: As 2nd row.

Rep these 4 rows.

6-stitch repeat

When ironing swatches or garments, lay piece wrong side up on a flat padded surface. Use a damp cloth between the knitted piece and the iron. For yarns that should not be ironed, steam the surface without touching the knitting.

Curvy Checks

Multiple of 8 + 5.

1st row (right side): K5, *p3, k5; rep from * to end.

2nd row: P5, *k3, p5; rep from * to end.

3rd and 4th rows: Rep the last 2 rows once more.

5th row: K1, p3, *k5, p3; rep from * to last st, k1.

6th row: P1, k3, *p5, k3; rep from * to last st, p1.

7th and 8th rows: Rep the last 2 rows once more.

Rep these 8 rows.

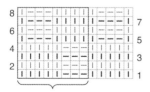

8-stitch repeat

Criss-Cross Cable Panel

Panel of 12 sts on a background of reverse St st.

1st row (wrong side): K1, p4, k2, p4, k1.

2nd row: [T3B, T3F] twice.

3rd row: P2, k2, p4, k2, p2.

4th row: [T3F, T3B] twice.

5th row: As 1st row.

6th row: P1, k4, p2, k4, p1.

7th row: As 1st row.

8th row: P1, C4B, p2, C4F, p1.

9th row: As 1st row.

10th row: As 2nd row.

11th row: As 3rd row.

12th row: K2, p2, C4F, p2, k2.

13th row: As 3rd row.

14th row: As 4th row.

15th row: As 1st row.

16th row: P1, C4F, p2, C4B, p1.

17th row: As 1st row.

18th row: As 6th row.

Rep these 18 rows.

Slanting Pillars

Panel of 8 sts on a background of reverse St st.

1st row (right side): K2, p4, k2.

2nd row: P2, k4, p2.

3rd row: C4F, C4B.

4th row: P8.

5th to 8th rows: Rep 1st and 2nd rows twice.

Rep these 8 rows.

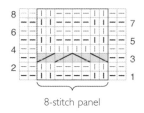

8-stitch panel

Crossed Diamond Cable

Multiple of 12 + 14.

1st row (right side): K4, C3B, C3F, *k6, C3B, C3F; rep from * to last 4 sts, k4.

2nd row and every alt row: Purl.

3rd row: K3, C3B, k2, C3F, *k4, C3B, k2, C3F; rep from * to last 3 sts, k3.

5th row: *K2, C3B, k4, C3F; rep from * to last 2 sts, k2.

7th row: K1, *C3B, k6, C3F; rep from * to last st, k1.

9th row: K11, *C4B, k8; rep from * to last 3 sts, k3.

11th row: K1, *C3F, k6, C3B; rep from * to last st, k1.

13th row: *K2, C3F, k4, C3B; rep from * to last 2 sts, k2.

15th row: K3, C3F, k2, C3B, *k4, C3F, k2, C3B; rep from * to last 3 sts, k3.

17th row: K4, C3F, C3B, *k6, C3F, C3B; rep from * to last

4 sts, k4.

19th row: K5, C4B, *k8, C4B; rep from * to last 5 sts, k5.

20th row: Purl.

Rep these 20 rows.

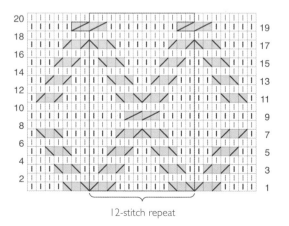

12-stitch repeat

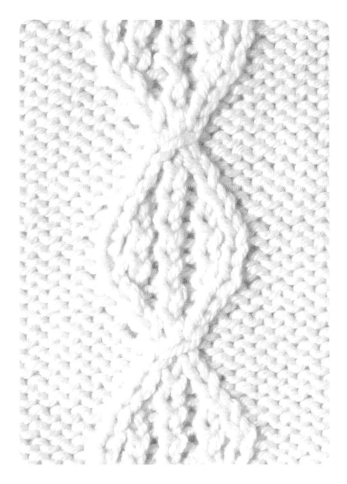

Tulip Cable II

Panel of 9 sts on a background of reverse St st.

1st row (right side): P2, T2B, KB1, T2F, p2.

2nd row: K2, p1, [k1, p1] twice, k2.

3rd row: P1, C2B, p1, KB1, p1, C2F, p1.

4th row: K1, p2, k1, p1, k1, p2, k1.

5th row: T2B, KB1, [p1, KB1] twice, T2F.

6th row: P1, [k1, p1] 4 times.

7th row: T2F, KB1, [p1, KB1] twice, T2B.

8th row: As 4th row.

9th row: P1, T2F, p1, KB1, p1, T2B, p1.

10th row: As 2nd row.

11th row: P2, T2F, KB1, T2B, p2.

12th row: K3, p3, k3.

13th row: P3, C3R, p3.

14th row: K3, p3, k3.

Rep these 14 rows.

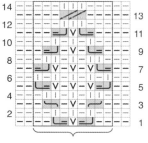

9-stitch panel

Ascending Spirals

Panel of 6 sts on a background of reverse St st.

1st row (right side): K6.

2nd row: P6.

3rd row: C6B.

4th row: P6.

5th and 6th rows: As 1st and 2nd rows.

Rep these 6 rows.

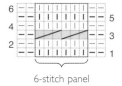

6-stitch panel

Vertical Zig-Zags

Multiple of 8 + 2.

1st row (right side): P5, T4R, *p4, T4R; rep from * to last st, p1.

2nd row: K2, *p3, k5; rep from * to end.

3rd row: *P4, T4R; rep from * to last 2 sts, p2.

4th row: K3, p3, *k5, p3; rep from * to last 4 sts, k4.

5th row: P3, T4R, *p4, T4R; rep from * to last 3 sts, p3.

6th row: K4, p3, *k5, p3; rep from * to last 3 sts, k3.

7th row: P2, *T4R, p4; rep from * to end.

8th row: *K5, p3; rep from * to last 2 sts, k2.

9th row: P1, *T4R, p4; rep from * to last st, p1.

10th row: K6, p3, *k5, p3; rep from * to last st, k1.

11th row: P1, *T4L, p4; rep from * to last st, p1.

12th row: As 8th row.

13th row: P2, *T4L, p4; rep from * to end.

14th row: As 6th row.

15th row: P3, T4L, *p4, T4L; rep from * to last 3 sts, p3.

16th row: As 4th row.

17th row: *P4, T4L; rep from * to last 2 sts, p2.

18th row: As 2nd row.

19th row: P5, T4L, *p4, T4L; rep from * to last st, p1.

20th row: K1, *p3, k5; rep from * to last st, k1.

Rep these 20 rows.

Note: This stitch is also very effective when worked as a panel of 10 or 18 sts on a background of reverse St st.

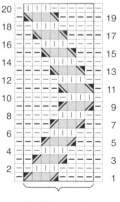

8-stitch repeat

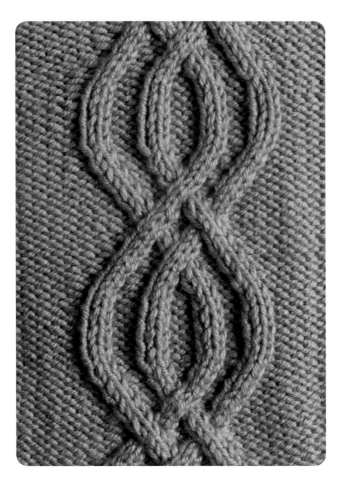

6th row: K2, p2, k3, p4, k3, p2, k2.

7th row: P2, T3F, p2, C4B, p2, T3B, p2.

8th row: K3, p2, k2, p4, k2, p2, k3.

9th row: P3, [T3F, T3B] twice, p3.

10th row: K4, p4, k2, p4, k4.

11th row: P4, C4F, p2, C4F, p4.

12th row: As 10th row.

13th row: P3, [T3B, T3F] twice, p3.

14th row: As 8th row.

15th row: P2, T3B, p2, C4B, p2, T3F, p2.

16th row: As 6th row.

17th row: P1, T3B, p2, T3B, T3F, p2, T3F, p1.

18th row: As 4th row.

19th row: T3B, p2, T3B, [p2, T3F] twice.

20th row: As 2nd row.

21st to 24th rows: Rep 1st and 2nd rows twice.

Rep these 24 rows.

Overlapping Ovals

Panel of 18 sts on a background of reverse St st.

1st row (right side): K2, p3, k2, p4, k2, p3, k2.

2nd row: P2, k3, p2, k4, p2, k3, p2.

3rd row: T3F, p2, T3F, [p2, T3B] twice.

4th row: K1, p2, k3, p2, k2, p2, k3, p2, k1.

5th row: P1, T3F, p2, T3F, T3B, p2, T3B, p1.

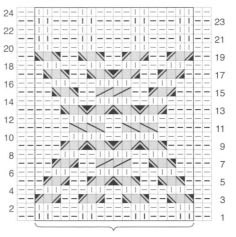

18-stitch panel

Slanting Trellis

Multiple of 4 + 3.

1st row (right side): P1, T2F, *p2, T2F; rep from * to last 4 sts, p4.

2nd row: K4, p1, *k3, p1; rep from * to last 2 sts, k2.

3rd row: *P2, T2F; rep from * to last 3 sts, p3.

4th row: K3, *p1, k3; rep from * to end.

5th row: P3, *T2F, p2; rep from * to end.

6th row: K2, p1, *k3, p1; rep from * to last 4 sts, k4.

7th row: P4, T2F, *p2, T2F; rep from * to last 5 sts, p5.

8th row: K1, p1, *k3, p1; rep from * to last 5 sts, k5.

Rep these 8 rows.

4-stitch repeat

Enclosed Seed Cable

Panel of 16 sts on a background of reverse St st.

1st row (right side): P4, C4R, C4L, p4.

2nd row: K4, p8, k4.

3rd row: P3, C4R, k2, C4L, p3.

4th row: K3, p10, k3.

5th row: P2, T4R, k4, T4L, p2.

6th row: K2, p3, k1, p4, k1, p3, k2.

7th row: P1, T4R, p1, C4B, p1, T4L, p1.

8th row: K1, p3, k2, p4, k2, p3, k1.

9th row: T4R, p2, k4, p2, T4L.

10th row: P3, k3, p4, k3, p3.

11th row: T4L, p2, k4, p2, T4R.

12th row: As 8th row.

13th row: P1, T4L, p1, C4B, p1, T4R, p1.

14th row: As 6th row.

15th row: P2, T4L, k4, T4R, p2.

16th row: K3, p10, k3.

17th row: P3, T4L, k2, T4R, p3.

18th row: K4, p8, k4.

19th row: P4, T4L, T4R, p4.

20th row: K5, p6, k5.

21st row: P5, C6B, p5.

22nd row: K5, p6, k5.

Rep these 22 rows.

Round Cable

Panel of 8 sts on a background of reverse St st.

1st row (right side): P2, k4, p2.

2nd row: K2, p4, k2.

3rd and 4th rows: Rep the last 2 rows once more.

5th row: T4B, T4F.

6th row: P2, k4, p2.

7th row: As 2nd row.

8th to 10th rows: Rep the last 2 rows once more then the 6th row again.

11th row: T4F, T4B.

12th row: As 2nd row.

Rep these 12 rows.

Use circular needles to take the strain out of knitting large projects. Holding the whole project on one straight needle puts strain on wrists—a circular needle will help distribute the weight better.

Giant Braid Cable

Panel of 18 sts on a background of reverse St st.

1st row (right side): K18.

2nd row: P18.

3rd row: K6, C12F.

4th row: P18.

5th to 10th rows: Rep 1st and 2nd rows 3 times.

11th row: C12B, k6.

12th row: P18.

13th to 16th rows: Rep 1st and 2nd rows twice.

Rep these 16 rows.

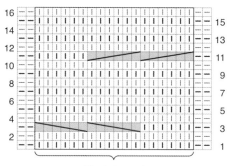

18-stitch panel

4-Stitch Cable

Panel of 4 sts on a background of reverse St st.

1st row (right side): Knit.

2nd row: Purl.

3rd row: C4B.

4th row: Purl.

Rep these 4 rows.

Note: The cable as given above twists to the right. To work the 4 st cable twisted to the left, work C4F instead of C4B in the 3rd row.

Climbing Arrow Cable

Panel of 24 sts on a background of reverse St st.

1th row (right side): K2, p4, T4F, p1, C2B, p1, T4B, p4, k2.

2nd row: P2, k6, [p2, k1] twice, p2, k6, p2.

3rd row: T4F, p4, T4F, T4B, p4, T4B.

4th row: K2, p2, k6, p4, k6, p2, k2.

5th row: P2, C4F, p4, T2F, T2B, p4, C4B, p2.

6th row: K2, p4, k5, p2, k5, p4, k2.

7th row: T4B, T4F, p3, C2B, p3, T4B, T4F.

8th row: P2, k4, [p2, k3] twice, p2, k4, p2.

Rep these 8 rows.

24-stitch panel

8-Stitch Cable

1st row (right side): Knit.

2nd row: Purl.

3rd and 4th rows: Rep the last 2 rows once more.

5th row: C8B.

6th row: Purl.

7th to 10th rows: Rep 1st and 2nd rows twice more.

Rep these 10 rows.

Note: The cable as given above twists to the right. To work the 8 st cable twisted to the left, work C8F instead of C8B in the 5th row.

Winding Cable

Panel of 8 sts on a background of reverse St st.

1st row (right side): K8.

2nd row: P8.

3rd row: C8B.

4th row: P8.

5th to 10th rows: Rep 1st and 2nd rows 3 times.

11th row: C8F.

12th row: P8.

13th to 16th rows: Rep 1st and 2nd rows twice.

Rep these 16 rows.

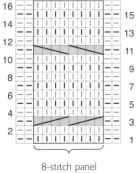

8-stitch panel

Cable with Ripples

Panel of 4 sts on a background of reverse St st.

1st row (right side): K4.

2nd row: P4.

3rd row: C4F.

4th row: P4.

Rep these 4 rows.

4-stitch panel

Pinched Cable

Panel of 3 sts on a background of reverse St st.

Special Abbreviation

T3RP (Twist 3 Right Purl) = slip next 2 sts onto cable needle and hold at back of work, knit next st from left-hand needle, then p1, k1 from cable needle.

1st row (right side): K1, p1, k1.

2nd row: PB1, k1, PB1.

3rd row: T3RP.

4th row: PB1, k1, PB1.

5th and 6th rows: As 1st and 2nd rows.

Rep these 6 rows.

3-stitch panel

Pillars with Spirals

Multiple of 7 + 2.

1st row (right side): P2, *k3, C2B, p2; rep from * to end.

2nd row and every alt row: K2, *p5, k2; rep from * to end.

3rd row: P2, *k2, C2B, k1, p2; rep from * to end.

5th row: P2, *k1, C2B, k2, p2; rep from * to end.

7th row: P2, *C2B, k3, p2; rep from * to end.

8th row: As 2nd row.

Rep these 8 rows.

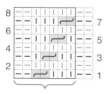

7-stitch repeat

Diamonds with Knots I

Panel of 16 sts on a background of reverse St st.

1st row (right side): P4, C4R, T4L, p4.

2nd row: K4, p3, k1, p4, k4.

3rd row: P3, C4R, p1, k1, T4L, p3.

4th row: K3, p3, k1, p1, k1, p4, k3.

5th row: P2, C4R, [p1, k1] twice, T4L, p2.

6th row: K2, p3, k1, [p1, k1] twice, p4, k2.

7th row: P1, C4R, [p1, k1] 3 times, T4L, p1.

8th row: K1, p3, k1, [p1, k1] 3 times, p4, k1.

9th row: C4R, [p1, k1] 4 times, T4L.

10th row: P3, k1, [p1, k1] 4 times, p4.

11th row: T4L, [k1, p1] 4 times, T4R.

12th row: As 8th row.

13th row: P1, T4L, [k1, p1] 3 times, T4R, p1.

14th row: As 6th row.

15th row: P2, T4L, [k1, p1] twice, T4R, p2.

16th row: As 4th row.

17th row: P3, T4L, k1, p1, T4R, p3.

18th row: As 2nd row.

19th row: P4, T4L, T4R, p4.

20th row: K5, p6, k5.

21st row: P5, C6B, p5.

22nd row: K5, p6, k5.

Rep these 22 rows.

Donut Cable

Panel of 16 sts on a background of reverse St st.

1st row (right side): K16.

2nd row: P16.

3rd row: C8B, C8F.

4th row: P16.

5th to 10th rows: Rep 1st and 2nd rows 3 times.

11th row: C8F, C8B.

12th row: P16.

13th to 16th rows: Rep 1st and 2nd rows twice.

Rep these 16 rows.

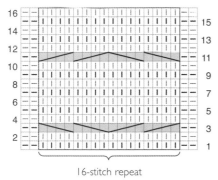

16-stitch repeat

Lattice Cable

Panel of 24 sts on a background of reverse St st.

1st row (right side): K2, p8, C4B, p8, k2.

2nd row: P2, k8, p4, k8, p2.

3rd row: T4F, p4, T4B, T4F, p4, T4B.

4th row: K2, [p2, k4] 3 times, p2, k2.

5th row: P2, T4F, T4B, p4, T4F, T4B, p2.

6th row: K4, p4, k8, p4, k4.

7th row: P4, C4B, p8, C4F, p4.

8th row: As 6th row.

9th row: P2, T4B, T4F, p4, T4B, T4F, p2.

10th row: As 4th row.

11th row: T4B, p4, T4F, T4B, p4, T4F.

12th row: As 2nd row.

Rep these 12 rows.

OXO Cable

Panel of 8 sts on a background of St st.

1st row (right side): Knit.

2nd row and every alt row: Purl.

3rd row: C4F, C4B.

5th row: Knit.

7th row: C4B, C4F.

9th row: Knit.

11th row: C4B, C4F.

13th row: Knit.

15th row: C4F, C4B.

16th row: Purl.

Rep these 16 rows.

Twisted Ladder Cable

Panel 12 sts on a background of reverse St st.

1st row (right side): T3F, p2, T3B, T3F, p1.

2nd row: K1, [yfrn, p2, pass yfrn over the 2 purled sts, k2] twice, yfrn, p2, pass yfrn over 2 purled sts, k1.

3rd row: P1, T3F, T3B, p2, T3F.

4th row: *Yfrn, p2, pass yfrn over the 2 purled sts*, k4; rep from * to * once more, yrn, p2, pass yrn over 2 purled sts, k2.

5th row: P2, C4B, p4, k2.

6th row: As 4th row.

7th row: P1, T3B, T3F, p2, T3B.

8th row: As 2nd row.

9th row: T3B, p2, T3F, T3B, p1.

10th row: K2, *yfrn, p2, pass yfrn over 2 purled sts*, yrn, p2, pass yrn over 2 purled sts, k4, rep from * to * once more.

11th row: K2, p4, C4F, p2.

12th row: As 10th row.

Rep these 12 rows.

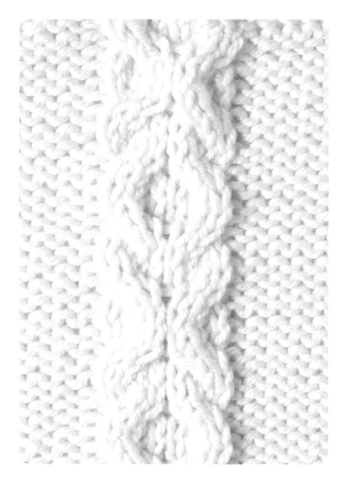

Linked Rings

Panel of 8 sts on a background of reverse St st.

1st row (right side): K8.

2nd row: P8.

3rd row: C4B, C4F.

4th row P8.

5th to 10th rows: Rep 1st to 4th rows once more, then 1st and 2nd rows again.

11th row: C4F, C4B.

12th row: P8.

13th and 14th rows: As 1st and 2nd rows.

15th and 16th rows: As 11th and 12th rows.

Rep these 16 rows.

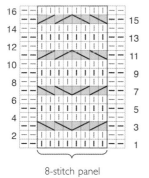

8-stitch panel

Small Double Cable

Panel of 8 sts on a background of reverse St st.

1st row (right side): Knit.

2nd row: Purl.

3rd and 4th rows: Rep the last 2 rows once more.

5th row: C4F, C4B.

6th row: Purl.

Rep these 6 rows.

Twist and Cable

Panel of 16 sts on a background of reverse St st.

1st row (wrong side): K4, p8, k4.

2nd row: P3, T2B, k6, T2F, p3.

3rd row: K3, p1, k1, p6, k1, p1, k3.

4th row: P2, T2B, p1, k6, p1, T2F, p2.

5th row: K2, p1, k2, p6, k2, p1, k2.

6th row: P1, T2B, p2, C6B, p2, T2F, p1.

7th row: K1, p1, k3, p6, k3, p1, k1.

8th row: T2B, p3, k6, p3, T2F.

9th row: P1, k4, p6, k4, p1.

10th row: T2F, p3, k6, p3, T2B.

11th row: As 7th row.

12th row: P1, T2F, p2, C6B, p2, T2B, p1.

13th row: As 5th row.

14th row: P2, T2F, p1, k6, p1, T2B, p2.

15th row: As 3rd row.

16th row: P3, T2F, k6, T2B, p3.

Rep these 16 rows.

Lazy Links

Multiple of 8 + 10.

Special Abbreviation

Cluster 6 = k2, p2, k2 from left-hand needle, slip these 6 sts onto a cable needle. Wrap yarn twice counterclockwise round these 6 sts. Slip sts back onto right-hand needle.

1st row (right side): P2, *k2, p2; rep from * to end.

2nd row and every alt row: K2, *p2, k2; rep from * to end.

3rd row: P2, *cluster 6, p2; rep from * to end.

5th row: As 1st row.

7th row: P2, k2, p2, *cluster 6, p2; rep from * to last 4 sts, k2, p2.

8th row: As 2nd row.

Rep these 8 rows.

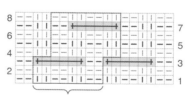

8-stitch repeat

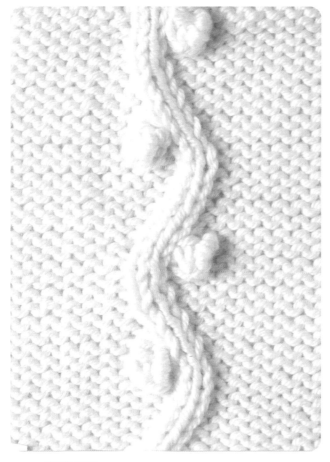

6-stitch panel

Alternating Bobbles

Panel of 6 sts on a background of reverse St st.

Special Abbreviation

MB#2 (Make Bobble number 2) – see page 263.

1st row (right side): P1, MB#2, p1, T3B.

2nd row: K1, p2, k3.

3rd row: P2, T3B, p1.

4th row: K2, p2, k2.

5th row: P1, T3B, p2.

6th row: K3, p2, k1.

7th row: T3B, p3.

8th row: K4, p2.

9th row: T3F, p1, MB#2, p1.

10th row: K3, p2, k1.

11th row: P1, T3F, p2.

12th row: K2, p2, k2.

13th row: P2, T3F, p1.

14th row: K1, p2, k3.

15th row: P3, T3F.

16th row: P2, k4.

Rep these 16 rows.

Slipped Wavy Cable

Panel of 3 sts on a background of reverse St st.

1st row (right side): Sl 1 purlwise, k2.

2nd row: P2, sl 1 purlwise.

3rd row: C3L.

4th row: Purl.

5th row: K2, sl 1 purlwise.

6th row: Sl 1 purlwise, p2.

7th row: C3R.

8th row: Purl.

Rep these 8 rows.

Cable and Twist Ripple

Panel of 9 sts on a background of reverse St st.

1st row (right side): T2F, T3B, p1, T3B.
2nd row: K1, p2, k2, p3, k1.
3rd row: P1, T3B, p1, C3B, p1.
4th row: K1, p3, k2, p2, k1.
5th row: T3B, p1, T3B, T2F.
6th row: P1, [k2, p2] twice.
7th row: [K2, p2] twice, k1.
8th row: As 6th row.
9th row: T3F, p1, T3F, T2B.
10th row: As 4th row.
11th row: P1, C3F, p1, T3F, p1.
12th row: As 2nd row.
13th row: T2B, T3F, p1, T3F.
14th row: [P2, k2] twice, p1.
15th row: K1, [p2, k2] twice.
16th row: As 14th row.

Rep these 16 rows.

Chalice Cable

Panel of 16 sts on a background of reverse St st.

1st row (right side): K1, [p2, k2] 3 times, p2, k1.

2nd row: P1, k2, [p2, k2] 3 times, p1.

3rd to 6th rows: Rep the last 2 rows twice more.

7th row: Slip next 4 sts onto cable needle and hold at back of work, k1, p2, k1 from left-hand needle, then k1, p2, k1 from cable needle, slip next 4 sts onto cable needle and hold at front of work, k1, p2, k1 from left-hand needle, then k1, p2, k1 from cable needle.

8th row: As 2nd row.

9th row: As 1st row.

10th row: As 2nd row.

Rep these 10 rows.

If accidental yarnovers are a problem for you, count the number of stitches on your needle every few rows.

Diamonds with Knots II

Panel of 11 sts on a background of reverse St st.

1st row (right side): P2, C3B, p1, C3F, p2.

2nd row: K2, p3, k1, p3, k2.

3rd row: P1, C3B, p1, k1, p1, C3F, p1.

4th row: K1, p3, k1, p1, k1, p3, k1.

5th row: C3B, p1, [k1, p1] twice, C3F.

6th row: P3, k1, [p1, k1] twice, p3.

7th row: K2, p1, [k1, p1] 3 times, k2.

8th row: P2, k1, [p1, k1] 3 times, p2.

9th row: T3F, p1, [k1, p1] twice, T3B.

10th row: K1, p2, k1, [p1, k1] twice, p2, k1.

11th row: P1, T3F, p1, k1, p1, T3B, p1.

12th row: K2, p2, k1, p1, k1, p2, k2.

13th row: P2, T3F, p1, T3B, p2.

14th row: K3, p2, k1, p2, k3.

15th row: P3, C5B, p3.

16th row: K3, p5, k3.

Rep these 16 rows.

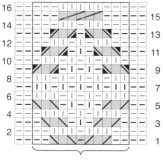

11-stitch panel

Interrupted Weave

Worked over 24 sts on a background of reverse St st.

1st row (right side): K1, p2, k3, p2, k2, p2, k9, p2, k1.

2nd row: [P1, k2] twice, p2, k2, p11, k2, p1.

3rd and 4th rows: Rep 1st and 2nd rows once more.

5th row: K1, p2, k3, p2, k2, p2, C8F, k1, p2, k1.

6th row: As 2nd row.

7th to 10th rows: Rep 1st and 2nd rows twice more.

11th row: K1, p2, k9, p2, k2, p2, k3, p2, k1.

12th row: P1, k2, p11, k2, p2, [k2, p1] twice.

13th and 14th rows: Rep 11th and 12th rows once more.

15th row: K1, p2, k1, C8F, p2, k2, p2, k3, p2, k1.

16th row: As 12th row.

17th to 20th rows: Rep 11th and 12th rows twice more.

Rep these 20 rows.

Double Cable

Worked over 12 sts.

Downwards Cable (shown on right)

1st row (right side): Knit.

2nd row: Purl.

3rd row: C6F, C6B.

4th row: Purl.

5th to 8th rows: Rep 1st and 2nd rows twice more.

Rep these 8 rows.

Upwards Cable (shown on left)

1st row (right side): Knit.

2nd row: Purl.

3rd row: C6B, C6F.

4th row: Purl.

5th to 8th rows: Rep 1st and 2nd rows twice more.

Rep these 8 rows.

Divided Bobble Cable II

Panel of 12 sts on a background of reverse St st.

Special Abbreviation

MB#8 (Make Bobble number 8) – see page 263.

1st row (right side): K2, [p1, k1] 5 times.

2nd row: [P1, k1] 5 times, p2.

3rd row: T4F, [p1, k1] 4 times.

4th row: [P1, k1] 4 times, p2, k2.

5th row: P2, T4F, [p1, k1] 3 times.

6th row: [P1, k1] 3 times, p2, k4.

7th row: P4, T4F, [p1, k1] twice.

8th row: [P1, k1] twice, p2, k6.

9th row: P1, MB#8, p4, T4F, p1, k1.

10th row: P1, k1, p2, k8.

11th row: P4, MB#8, p3, T4F.

12th row: P2, k10.

13th row: P1, MB#8, p5, MB#8, p2, k2.

14th row: P2, k10.

15th row: P4, MB#8, p3, T4BP.

16th row: As 10th row.

17th row: P1, MB#8, p4, T4BP, p1, k1.

18th row: As 8th row.

19th row: P4, T4BP, [p1, k1] twice.

20th row: As 6th row.

21st row: P2, T4BP, [p1, k1] 3 times.

22nd row: As 4th row.

23rd row: T4BP, [p1, k1] 4 times.

24th row: As 2nd row.

Rep these 24 rows.

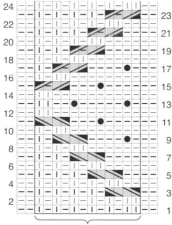

12-stitch panel

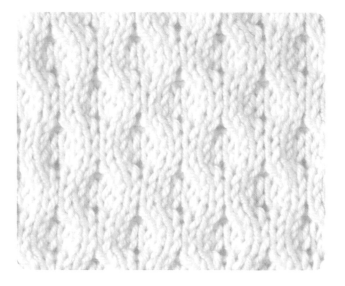

Woven Circles 1

Multiple of 6 + 2.

1st row (right side): Knit.

2nd row and every alt row: Purl.

3rd row: K1, *C3B, C3F; rep from * to last st, k1.

5th row: Knit.

7th row: K1, *C3F, C3B; rep from * to last st, k1.

8th row: Purl.

Rep these 8 rows.

Note: This stitch is also very effective when worked as a panel with a multiple of 6 sts on a background of reverse St st.

Linking Cables

Multiple of 16 + 16.

1st row (right side): P2, k4, *p4, k4; rep from * to last 2 sts, p2.

2nd row: K2, p4, *k4, p4; rep from * to last 2 sts, k2.

3rd row: P2, C4F, p4, C4B, *p4, C4F, p4, C4B; rep from * to last 2 sts, p2.

4th row: As 2nd row.

5th to 8th rows: Rep the last 4 rows once more.

9th row: P1, T3B, T4F, T4B, T3F, *p2, T3B, T4F, T4B, T3F; rep from * to last st, p1.

10th row: K1, p2, k3, p4, k3, p2, *k2, p2, k3, p4, k3, p2; rep from * to last st, k1.

11th row: P1, k2, p3, C4B, p3, k2, *p2, k2, p3, C4B, p3, k2; rep from * to last st, p1.

12th row: As 10th row.

13th row: P1, T3F, T4B, T4F, T3B, *p2, T3F, T4B, T4F, T3B; rep from * to last st, p1.

14th row: As 2nd row.

15th row: P2, C4B, p4, C4F, *p4, C4B, p4, C4F; rep from * to last 2 sts, p2.

16th row: As 2nd row.

17th row: As 1st row.

18th to 24th rows: Rep the last 4 rows once more, then 14th, 15th and 16th rows again.

25th row: P1, T3B, T3F, p2, T3B, *T4F, T4B, T3F, p2, T3B; rep from * to last 4 sts, T3F, p1.

26th row: K1, p2, [k2, p2] twice, *k3, p4, k3, p2, k2, p2; rep from * to last 5 sts, k2, p2, k1.

27th row: P1, k2, [p2, k2] twice, *p3, C4F, p3, k2, p2, k2; rep from * to last 5 sts, p2, k2, p1.

28th row: As 26th row.

29th row: P1, T3F, T3B, p2, T3F, *T4B, T4F, T3B, p2, T3F; rep from * to last 4 sts, T3B, p1.

30th to 32nd rows: As 2nd to 4th rows.

Rep these 32 rows.

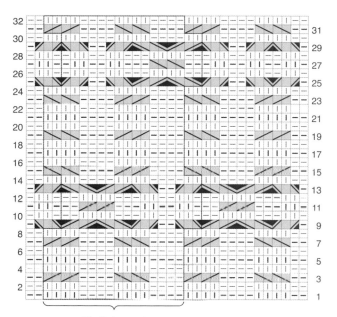

16-stitch repeat

Open Ring Cable

Panel of 10 sts on a background of reverse St st.

1st row (right side): P1, k8, p1.

2nd row: K1, p8, k1.

3rd row: P1, C4B, C4F, p1.

4th row: As 2nd row.

5th and 6th rows: As 1st and 2nd rows.

7th row: P1, T4B, T4F, p1.

8th row: K1, p2, k4, p2, k1.

9th row: T3B, p4, T3F.

10th row: P2, k6, p2.

11th row: K2, p6, k2.

12th row: P2, k6, p2.

13th row: T3F, p4, T3B.

14th row: As 8th row.

15th row: P1, C4F, C4B, p1.

16th row: K1, p8, k1.

Rep these 16 rows.

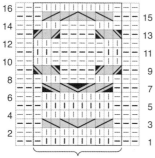

10-stitch panel

Interlocking Twist

Worked over 27 sts.

1st row (right side): K5, p1, k6, p3, k6, p1, k5.

2nd row: P5, k1, p6, k3, p6, k1, p5.

3rd row: K5, p1, C6B, p3, C6F, p1, k5.

4th row: As 2nd row.

5th to 10th row: Rep 1st to 4th rows once more, then 1st and 2nd rows again.

11th row: C12F, p3, C12B.

12th row: P6, k1, p5, k3, p5, k1, p6.

13th row: K6, p1, k5, p3, k5, p1, k6.

14th row: As 12th row.

15th row: C6F, p1, k5, p3, k5, p1, C6B.

16th row: As 12th row.

17th to 30th rows: Rep 13th to 16th rows 3 times more, then 13th and 14th rows again.

31st row: C12B, p3, C12F.

32nd row: As 2nd row.

33rd to 40th rows: Rep 1st to 4th rows twice.

Rep these 40 rows.

Vertical Curved Stripes

Multiple of 6 + 2.

1st row (right side): P2, *k4, p2; rep from * to end.

2nd row and every alt row: K2, *p4, k2; rep from * to end.

3rd row: P2, *C4B, p2; rep from * to end.

5th row: As 1st row.

7th row: P2, *C4F, p2; rep from * to end.

8th row: As 2nd row.

Rep these 8 rows.

6-stitch repeat

Braid Cable

Panel of 9 sts on a background of reverse St st.

1st row (right side): T2L, p2, T2R, T2L, p1.

2nd row: K1, [PB1, k2] twice, PB1, k1.

3rd row: P1, T2L, T2R, p2, T2L.

4th row: PB1, k4, [PB1] twice, k2.

5th row: P2, slip next st onto cable needle and hold at back of work, KB1 from left hand needle, then KB1 from cable needle, p4, KB1.

6th row: As 4th row.

7th row: P1, T2R, T2L, p2, T2R.

8th row: As 2nd row.

9th row: T2R, p2, T2L, T2R, p1.

10th row: K2, [PB1] twice, k4, PB1.

11th row: KB1, p4, slip next st onto cable needle and hold at front of work, KB1 from left-hand needle, then KB1 from cable needle, p2.

12th row: As 10th row.

Rep these 12 rows.

Filled Arrow Cable

Panel of 17 sts on a background of reverse St st.

1st row (right side): K2, p4, k2, p1, k2, p4, k2.

2nd row: K6, p2, k1, p2, k6.

3rd row: P6, T5BP, p6.

4th row: As 2nd row.

5th row: P5, T3B, k1, T3F, p5.

6th row: K5, p2, k1, p1, k1, p2, k5.

7th row: P4, T3B, k1, p1, k1, T3F, p4.

8th row: K4, p2, k1, [p1, k1] twice, p2, k4.

9th row: P3, T3B, k1, [p1, k1] twice, T3F, p3.

10th row: K3, p2, k1, [p1, k1] 3 times, p2, k3.

11th row: P2, T3B, k1, [p1, k1] 3 times, T3F, p2.

12th row: K2, p2, k1, [p1, k1] 4 times, p2, k2.

13th row: P1, T3B, k1, [p1, k1] 4 times, T3F, p1.

14th row: K1, p2, k1, [p1, k1] 5 times, p2, k1.

15th row: T3B, k1, [p1, k1] 5 times, T3F.

16th row: P2, k1, [p1, k1] 6 times, p2.

Rep these 16 rows.

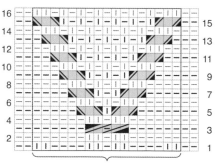

17-stitch panel

Cable Arrows

Panel of 8 sts on a background of reverse St st.

1st row (right side): Knit.

2nd row: Purl.

3rd row: P1, T3B, T3F, p1.

4th row: K1, p2, k2, p2, k1.

5th row: T3B, p2, T3F.

6th row: P2, k4, p2.

Rep these 6 rows.

To avoid knots in the middle of a row, check that there is enough yarn at the end of the row (approximately three times the swatch width/garment width). If there is not, leave a tail which can be woven in to the side seams later.

Woven Circles II

Multiple of 8 + 2.

1st row (right side): P3, k4, *p4, k4; rep from * to last 3 sts, k3.

2nd row: K3, p4, *k4, p4; rep from * to last 3 sts, k3.

3rd row: P1, *T4B, T4F; rep from * to last st, p1.

4th row: K1, p2, *k4, p4; rep from * to last 3 sts, p2, k1.

5th row: P1, k2, p4, *k4, p4; rep from * to last 3 sts, k2, p1.

6th row: As 4th row.

7th row: P1, *T4F, T4B; rep from * to last st, p1.

8th row: As 2nd row.

Rep these 8 rows.

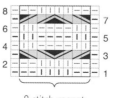

8-stitch repeat

Cable and Box Panel

Panel of 8 sts on a background of reverse St st.

1st row (right side): Knit.

2nd row: Purl.

3rd row: C8F.

4th to 7th rows: Work 4 rows in st st, starting purl.

8th row: P2, k4, p2.

9th row: K2, p4, k2.

10th to 13th rows: Rep the last 2 rows twice more.

14th to 16th rows: Work 3 rows in St st, starting purl.

Rep these 16 rows.

Triple Rib Cable

Worked over 5 sts.

Cable to the Right (shown on right)

1st row (right side): KB1, [p1, KB1] twice.

2nd row: PB1, [k1, PB1] twice.

3rd to 6th rows: Rep these 2 rows twice more.

7th row: Slip first 2 sts onto a cable needle and hold at back of work, work [KB1, p1, KB1] from left-hand needle, then work [p1, KB1] from cable needle.

8th row: As 2nd row.

9th to 14th rows: Rep 1st and 2nd rows 3 times more. Rep these 14 rows.

Cable to the Left (shown on left)

1st row (right side): KB1, [p1, KB1] twice.

2nd row: PB1, [k1, PB1] twice.

3rd to 6th rows: Rep these 2 rows twice more.

7th row: Slip first 3 sts onto a cable needle and hold at front of work, work [KB1, p1] from left-hand needle, then work [KB1, p1, KB1] from cable needle.

8th row: As 2nd row.

9th to 14th rows: Rep 1st and 2nd rows 3 times more. Rep these 14 rows.

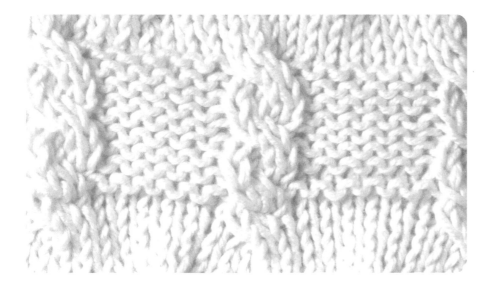

Ridge and Cable Stripes

Multiple of 10 + 8.

1st to 5th rows: Work 5 rows in St st, starting purl (1st row is wrong side).

6th row K7, C4B, *k6, C4B; rep from * to last 7 sts, k7.

7th row: K7, p4, *k6, p4; rep from * to last 7 st, k7.

8th row: P7, k4, *p6, k4; rep from * to last 7 sts, p7.

9th row: As 7th row.

10th row: P7, C4B, *p6, C4B; rep from * to last 7 sts, p7.

11th row: As 7th row.

12th row: As 8th row.

13th row: As 7th row.

14th row: As 6th row.

15th to 19th rows: Work 5 rows in St st, starting purl.

20th row: K2, C4F, *k6, C4F; rep from * to last 2 sts, k2.

21st row: K2, p4, *k6, p4; rep from * to last 2 sts, k2.

22nd row: P2, k4, *p6, k4; rep from * to last 2 sts, p2.

23rd row: As 21st row.

24th row: P2, C4F, *p6, C4F; rep from * to last 2 sts, p2.

25th row: As 21st row.

26th row: As 22nd row.

27th row: As 21st row.

28th row: As 20th row.

Rep these 28 rows.

Branched Cable I

Panel of 10 sts on a background of reverse St st.

1st row (right side): P3, C4F, p3.

2nd row: K3, p4, k3.

3rd row: P2, C3B, C3F, p2.

4th row: K2, p6, k2.

5th row: P1, C3B, k2, C3F, p1.

6th row: K1, p8, k1.

7th row: C3B, k4, C3F.

8th row: Purl.

Rep these 8 rows.

Note: The cable as given here crosses to the left. To work the cable crossed to the right, work C4B instead of C4F in the 1st row.

Textured Cable II

Panel of 15 sts on a background of reverse St st.

1st row (right side): P4, C3B, p1, C3F, p4.

2nd row: K4, p3, k1, p3, k4.

3rd row: P3, C3B, p1, k1, p1, C3F, p3.

4th row: K3, p3, k1, p1, k1, p3, k3.

5th row: P2, C3B, p1, [k1, p1] twice, C3F, p2.

6th row: K2, p3, k1, [p1, k1] twice, p3, k2.

7th row: P1, C3B, p1, [k1, p1] 3 times, C3F, p1.

8th row: K1, p3, k1, [p1, k1] 3 times, p3, k1.

9th row: C3B, p1, [k1, p1] 4 times, C3F.

10th row: P3, k1, [p1, k1] 4 times, p3.

11th row: K2, p1, [k1, p1] 5 times, k2

12th row: P2, k1, [p1, k1] 5 times, p2.

13th row: T3F, p1, [k1, p1] 4 times, T3B.

14th row: K1, p2, k1, [p1, k1] 4 times, p2, k1.

15th row: P1, T3F, p1, [k1, p1] 3 times, T3B, p1.

16th row: K2, p2, k1, [p1, k1] 3 times, p2, k2.

17th row: P2, T3F, p1, [k1, p1] twice, T3B, p2.

18th row: K3, p2, k1, [p1, k1] twice, p2, k3.

19th row: P3, T3F, p1, k1, p1, T3B, p3.

20th row: K4, p2, k1, p1, k1, p2, k4.

21st row: P4, T3F, p1, T3B, p4.

22nd row: K5, p2, k1, p2, k5.

23rd row: P5, C5B, p5.

24th row: K5, p5, k5.

Rep these 24 rows.

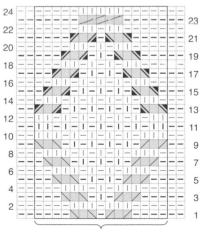

15-stitch panel

Garter and Stockinette Stitch Cable

Panel of 8 sts on a background of reverse St st.

1st row (right side): Knit.

2nd row: P4, k4.

3rd to 6th rows: Rep the last 2 rows twice more.

7th row: C8B.

8th row: K4, p4.

9th row: Knit.

10th to 18th rows: Rep the last 2 rows 4 times more, then the 8th row again.

19th row: C8B.

20th row: As 2nd row.

21st row: Knit.

22nd to 24th rows: Rep the last 2 rows once more then the 20th row again.

Rep these 24 rows.

Hanging Bobbles

Panel of 11 sts on a background of reverse St st.

Special Abbreviation

MB#3 (Make Bobble number 3) – see page 263.

1st row (right side): P11.

2nd row: K11.

3rd row: P5, MB#3, p5.

4th row: K5, PB1, k5.

5th row: P2, MB#3, p2, KB1, p2, MB#3, p2.

6th row: K2, [PB1, k2] 3 times.

7th row: MB#3, p1, T2F, p1, KB1, p1, T2B, p1, MB#3.

8th row: PB1, k2, PB1, [k1, PB1] twice, k2, PB1.

9th row: T2F, p1, T2F, KB1, T2B, p1, T2B.

10th row: K1, T2BW, k1, [PB1] 3 times, k1, T2FW, k1.

11th row: P2, T2F, M1P, sl 1, k2tog, psso, M1P, T2B, p2.

12th row: K3, T2BW, PB1, T2FW, k3.

13th row: P4, M1P, sl 1, k2tog, psso, M1P, p4.

14th row: K5, PB1, k5.

15th row: P11.

16th row: K11.

Rep these 16 rows.

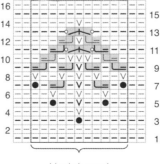

11-stitch panel

Bulbus Cable

Panel of 6 sts on a background of reverse St st.

Special Abbreviation

C6LR (Cross 6 Left and Right) = slip next 2 sts onto cable needle and hold at back of work, slip next 2 sts onto 2nd cable needle and hold at front of work, knit next 2 sts from left-hand needle then knit the 2 sts from 2nd cable needle, then knit the 2 sts from 1st cable needle.

1st row (right side): Knit.

2nd row: Purl.

3rd row: C6LR.

4th row: Purl.

5th row: Knit.

6th and 7th rows: Rep the last 2 rows once more.

8th row: Purl.

Rep these 8 rows.

Ascending Tulips

Panel of 12 sts on a background of reverse St st.

1st row (right side): K12.

2nd row: P12.

3rd row: C6B, C6F.

4th row: P12.

5th and 6th rows: As 1st and 2nd rows.

Rep these 6 rows.

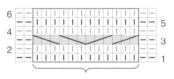

12-stitch panel

Branched Cable II

Panel of 10 sts on a background of reverse St st.

1st row (right side): P3, C4B, p3.

2nd row: K3, p4, k3.

3rd row: P2, T3B, T3F, p2.

4th row: [K2, p2] twice, k2.

5th row: P1, T3B, p2, T3F, p1.

6th row: K1, p2, k4, p2, k1.

7th row: T3B, p4, T3F.

8th row: P2, k6, p2.

Rep these 8 rows.

Note: The cable as given here crosses to the right. To work the cable crossed to the left, work C4F instead of C4B in the 1st row.

Knotted Cable

Panel of 6 sts on a background of reverse St st.

1st row (right side): K2, p2, k2.

2nd and every alt row: P2, k2, p2.

3rd row: C6.

5th, 7th and 9th rows: K2, p2, k2.

10th row: As 2nd row.

Rep these 10 rows.

Folded Cable II

Panel of 6 sts on a background of reverse St st.

Downwards Cable (shown on right)

1st row (right side): Knit.

2nd row: Purl.

3rd and 4th rows: Rep 1st and 2nd rows once more.

5th row: C3L, C3R.

6th row: Purl.

7th to 12th rows: Rep 5th and 6th rows twice more, then 1st and 2nd rows once more.

Rep these 12 rows.

Upwards Cable (shown on left)

1st row (right side): Knit.

2nd row: Purl.

3rd and 4th rows: Rep 1st and 2nd rows once more.

5th row: C3R, C3L.

6th row: Purl.

7th to 12th rows: Rep 5th and 6th rows twice more, then 1st and 2nd rows once more.

Rep these 12 rows.

Cable with Bridge

Panel of 9 sts on a background of reverse St st.

Special Abbreviation

C9X (Cable 9X) = slip next 3 sts onto a cable needle and hold at back of work, slip following 3 sts onto 2nd cable needle and hold at front of work, knit next 3 sts from left-hand needle, knit the 3 sts from 2nd cable needle, then the 3 sts from 1st cable needle.

1st row (right side): K9.

2nd row: P9.

3rd and 4th rows: Rep 2st and 2nd rows once more.

5th row: C9X.

6th row: P9.

7th to 16th rows: Rep 1st and 2nd rows 5 times.

Rep these 16 rows.

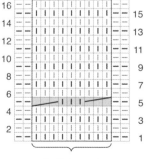

9-stitch panel

Woven Circles III

Multiple of 8 + 2.

1st row (right side): Knit.

2nd row: Purl.

3rd row: K1, *C4B, C4F; rep from * to last st, k1.

4th row: Purl.

5th and 6th rows: As 1st and 2nd rows.

7th row: K1, *C4F, C4B; rep from * to last st, k1.

8th row: Purl.

Rep these 8 rows.

Note: This stitch is also very effective when worked as a panel with a multiple of 8 sts on a background of reverse St st.

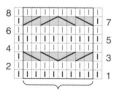

8-stitch repeat

Cable Rope

Panel of 8 sts on a background of reverse St st.

Special Abbreviations

T4BR (Twist 4 Back) = slip next st onto cable needle and hold back of work, knit next 3 sts from left-hand needle, then purl st from cable needle.

T4FL (Twist 4 Front) = slip next 3 sts onto cable needle and hold at front of work, purl next st from left-hand needle then knit sts from cable needle.

1st row (wrong side): K1, p6, k1.

2nd row: P1, k6, p1.

3rd row: As 1st row.

4th row: P1, C6B, p1.

5th row: As 1st row.

6th row: T4BR, T4FL.

7th row: P3, k2, p3.

8th row: K3, p2, k3.

9th to 19th rows: Rep the last 2 rows 5 times more then the 7th row again.

20th row: TF4L, T4BR.

21st to 26th rows: Rep the first 4 rows once more, then 1st and 2nd rows again.

Rep these 26 rows.

Slipped 5-Stitch Cable Braid

Panel of 5 sts on a background of reverse St st.

Downwards Braid (shown on right)

1st row (right side): Sl 1 purlwise, k4.

2nd row: P4, sl 1 purlwise.

3rd row: C3L, k2.

4th row: Purl.

5th row: K4, sl 1 purlwise.

6th row: Sl 1 purlwise, p4.

7th row: K2, C3R.

8th row: Purl.

Rep these 8 rows.

Upwards Braid (shown on left)

1st row (right side): K2, sl 1 purlwise, k2.

2nd row: P2, sl 1 purlwise, p2.

3rd row: K2, C3L.

4th row: Purl.

5th and 6th rows: Rep 1st and 2nd rows once.

7th row: C3R, k2.

8th row: Purl.

Rep these 8 rows.

Ionian Cables

Panel of 14 sts on a background of reverse St st.

1st row (right side): K4, p2, k2, p2, k4.

2nd row: P4, k2, p2, k2, p4.

3rd to 8th rows: Rep these 2 rows 3 times more.

9th row: C4F, p2, k2, p2, C4B.

10th row: As 2nd row.

11th row: K2, C4F, k2, C4B, k2.

12th row: Purl.

13th row: K4, p1, T2F, T2B, p1, k4.

14th row: As 2nd row.

15th row: As 1st row.

16th row: As 2nd row.

Rep these 16 rows.

Use a yarn needle to weave yarn ends into stitches on the wrong side.

Open Cable with Bobbles

Panel of 5 sts on a background of reverse St st.

Special Abbreviations

T5R (Twist 5 Right) = slip next 4 sts onto cable needle and hold at back of work, k1 from left-hand needle, then p3, k1 from cable needle.

T5L (Twist 5 Left) = slip next st onto cable needle and hold at front of work, k1, p3 from left-hand needle, then k1 from cable needle.

1st row (right side): T5R.

2nd row: P1, k3, p1.

3rd row: K1, p3, k1.

4th to 6th rows: Rep 2nd and 3rd rows once more then 2nd row again.

7th row: K1, p1, MB, p1, k1.

8th to 12th rows: Rep 2nd and 3rd rows twice more, then 2nd row again.

Rep these 12 rows.

Interlocking Crosses

Panel of 24 sts on a background of reverse St st.

1st row (right side): P2, C4B, [p4, C4B] twice, p2.

2nd row: K2, p4, [k4, p4] twice, k2.

3rd row: P1, T3B, [T4F, T4B] twice, T3F, p1.

4th row: K1, p2, k3, p4, k4, p4, k3, p2, k1.

5th row: T3B, p3, C4F, p4, C4F, p3, T3F.

6th row: P2, k4, [p4, k4] twice, p2.

7th row: K2, p3, T3B, T4F, T4B, T3F, p3, k2.

8th row: [P2, k3] twice, p4, [k3, p2] twice.

9th row: [K2, p3] twice, C4B, [p3, k2] twice.

10th row: As 8th row.

11th row: K2, p3, T3F, T4B, T4F, T3B, p3, k2.

12th row: As 6th row.

13th row: T3F, p3, C4F, p4, C4F, p3, T3B.

14th row: As 4th row.

15th row: P1, T3F, [T4B, T4F] twice, T3B, p1.

16th row: As 2nd row.

Rep these 16 rows.

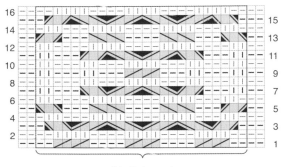

24-stitch panel

6-Stitch Slipped Double Cable

Panel of 6 sts on a background of reverse St st.

Downwards Cable (shown on left)

1st row (right side): Sl 1 purlwise, k4, sl 1 purlwise.

2nd row: Sl 1 purlwise, p4, sl 1 purlwise.

3rd and 4th rows: Rep 1st and 2nd rows once more.

5th row: C3L, C3R.

6th row: Purl.

Rep these 6 rows.

Upwards Cable (shown on right)

1st row (right side): K2, [sl 1 purlwise] twice, k2.

2nd row: P2, [sl 1 purlwise] twice, p2.

3rd and 4th rows: Rep 1st and 2nd rows once more.

5th row: C3R, C3L.

6th row: Purl.

Rep these 6 rows.

Big Wavy Cable Pattern

Panel of 16 sts on a background of reverse St st.

1st row (right side): P2, k4, p4, k4, p2.

2nd row: K2, p4, k4, p4, k2.

3rd row: P2, C4F, p4, C4B, p2.

4th row: As 2nd row.

5th to 8th rows: Rep the last 4 rows once more.

9th row: [T4B, T4F] twice.

10th row: P2, k4, p4, k4, p2.

11th row: K2, p4, k4, p4, k2.

12th row: As 10th row.

13th row: [T4F, T4B] twice.

14th row: As 2nd row.

15th row: P2, C4B, p4, C4F, p2.

16th row: As 2nd row.

17th row: As 1st row.

18th row: As 2nd row.

19th to 24th rows: Rep the last 4 rows once more, then first 2 rows again.

25th row: As 9th row.

26th row: As 10th row.

27th row: As 11th row.

28th row: As 10th row.

29th row: As 13th row.

30th row: As 2nd row.

31st row: As 3rd row.

32nd row: As 2nd row.

Rep these 32 rows.

Little Pearl Cable

Panel of 4 sts on a back ground of St st.

1st row (right side): C2F, C2B.

2nd row: Purl.

3rd row: C2B, C2F.

4th row: Purl.

Rep these 4 rows.

When knitting from a chart, make photocopies of the chart and use a highlighter pen to mark across each RS row after you complete it. Not only does this help you keep your place, but it makes it easy for your eyes to follow the right row of the chart.

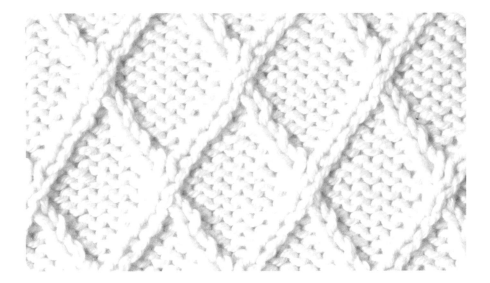

Diamond Lattice

Multiple of 8 + 4.

1st row (right side): P5, C2B, *p6, C2B; rep from * to last 5 sts, p5.

2nd row: K5, p2, *k6, p2; rep from * to last 5 sts, k5.

3rd row: P4, *T2B, T2F, p4; rep from * to end.

4th row: K4, *p1, k2, p1, k4; rep from * to end.

5th row: P3, *T2B, p2, T2F, p2; rep from * to last st, p1.

6th row: K3, *p1, k4, p1, k2; rep from * to last st, k1.

7th row: P2, *T2B, p4, T2F; rep from * to last 2 sts, p2.

8th row: K1, p2, *k6, p2; rep from * to last st, k1.

9th row: P1, C2B, *p6, C2B; rep from * to last st, p1.

10th row: As 8th row.

11th row: P2, *T2F, p4, T2B; rep from * to last 2 sts, p2.

12th row: As 6th row.

13th row: P3, *T2F, p2, T2B, p2; rep from * to last st, p1.

14th row: As 4th row.

15th row: P4, *T2F, T2B, p1; rep from * to end.

16th row: As 2nd row.

Rep these 16 rows.

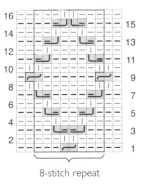

8-stitch repeat

Curved Diamond Cable

Panel of 12 sts on a background of reverse St st.

1st row (right side): P3, C3B, C3F, p3.

2nd row: K3, p6, k3.

3rd row: P2, T3B, C2B, T3F, p2.

4th row: K2, p2, [k1, p2] twice, k2.

5th row: P1, T3B, p1, C2B, p1, T3F, p1.

6th row: K1, p2, [k2, p2] twice, k1.

7th row: T3B, p2, C2B, p2, T3F.

8th row: P2, [k3, p2] twice.

9th row: T3F, p2, C2B, p2, T3B.

10th row: As 6th row.

11th row: P1, T3F, p1, C2B, p1, T3B, p1.

12th row: As 4th row.

13th row: P2, T3F, C2B, T3B, p2.

14th row: K3, p6, k3.

15th row: P3, T3F, T3B, p3.

16th row: K4, p4, k4.

17th row: P4, k4, p4.

18th row: K4, p4, k4.

Rep these 18 rows.

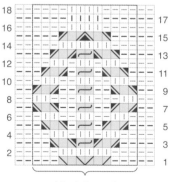

12-stitch panel

Cable with Lace Detail

Multiple of 12 + 2.

1st row (right side): Knit.

2nd and every alt row: Purl.

3rd row: K1, *C4B, k4, C4F; rep from * to last st, k1.

5th row: Knit.

7th row: K3, C4F, C4B, *k4, C4F, C4B; rep from * to last 3 sts, k3.

8th row: Purl.

Rep these 8 rows.

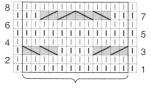

12-stitch repeat

Bold Diagonals I

Multiple of 8 + 5.

1st row (right side): P5, *T4R, p4; rep from * to end.

2nd row: K5, *p3, k5; rep from * to end.

3rd row: *P4, T4R; rep from * to last 5 sts, p5.

4th row: K6, p3, *k5, p3; rep from * to last 4 sts, k4.

5th row: P3, *T4R, p4; rep from * to last 2 sts, p2.

6th row: K7, p3, *k5, p3; rep from * to last 3 sts, k3.

7th row: P2, *T4R, p4; rep from * to last 3 sts, p3.

8th row: K8, p3, *k5, p3; rep from * to last 2 sts, k2.

9th row: P1, *T4R, p4; rep from * to last 4 sts, p4.

10th row: K9, p3, *k5, p3; rep from * to last st, k1.

11th row: P8, T4R, *p4, T4R; rep from * to last st, p1.

12th row: K2, *p3, k5; rep from * to last 3 sts, k3.

13th row: P7, T4R, *p4, T4R; rep from * to last 2 sts, p2.

14th row: K3, *p3, k5; rep from * to last 2 sts, k2.

15th row: P6, T4R, *p4, T4R; rep from * to last 3 sts, p3.

16th row: K4, *p3, k5; rep from * to last st, k1.

Rep these 16 rows.

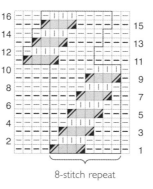

8-stitch repeat

Wavy Cable Pattern

Panel 14 sts on a background of reverse St st.

1st row (wrong side): K5, p4, k5.

2nd row: P5, C4B, p5.

3rd row: As 1st row.

4th row: P4, T3B, T3F, p4.

5th row: K4, p2, k2, p2, k4.

6th row: P2, T4B, p2, T4F, p2.

7th row: K2, p2, k6, p2, k2.

8th row: P2, T4F, p2, T4B, p2.

9th row: As 5th row.

10th row: P4, T3F, T3B, p4.

11th and 13th rows: As 1st row.

12th row: As 2nd row.

14th row: P5, k4, p5.

15th row: As 1st row.

16th row: As 2nd row.

17th row: As 1st row.

18th row: As 14th row.

Rep these 18 rows.

Cable Squares

Multiple of 12 + 2.

1st row (right side): [P1, k1] twice, p1, k5, *p1, [k1, p1] 3 times, k5; rep from * to last 4 sts, [p1, k1] twice.

2nd row: [K1, p1] twice, k1, p5, *[k1, p1] 3 times, k1, p5; rep from * to last 4 sts, [k1, p1] twice.

3rd row: P1, [k1, p1] twice, *C4B, [k1, p1] 4 times; rep from * to last 9 sts, C4B, k1, [p1, k1] twice.

4th row: As 2nd row.

5th to 12th rows: Rep the last 4 rows twice more.

13th row: Knit.

14th row: Purl.

15th row: K1, *C4B; rep from * to last st, k1.

16th row: Purl.

Rep these 16 rows.

Turning Cable

Panel of 12 sts on a background of reverse St st.

1st row (right side): K12.

2nd row: P12.

3rd row: C12B.

4th row: P12.

5th to 10th rows: Rep 1st and 2nd rows 3 times.

11th row: K2, C8B, k2.

12th row: P12.

13th to 18th rows: Rep 1st and 2nd rows 3 times.

19th to 20th rows: As 11th and 12th rows.

21st to 24th rows: Rep 1st and 2nd rows twice.

Rep these 24 rows.

Double Snakey Cable

Panel of 8 sts on a background or reverse St st.

1st row (right side): Knit.

2nd row: Purl.

3rd row: C4B, C4F.

4th row: Purl.

5th and 6th rows: Rep 1st and 2nd rows once more.

7th row: C4F, C4B.

8th row: Purl.

Rep these 8 rows.

Bold Diagonals II

Multiple of 8 + 5.

1st row (right side): *P4, T4L; rep from * to last 5 sts, p5.

2nd row: K5, *p3, k5; rep from * to end.

3rd row: P5, *T4l, p4; rep from * to end.

4th row: K4, *p3, k5; rep from * to last st, k1.

5th row: P6, T4L, *p4, T4L; rep from * to last 3 sts, p3.

6th row: K3, *p3, k5; rep from * to last 2 sts, k2.

7th row: P7, T4L, *p4, T4L; rep from * to last 2 sts, p2.

8th row: K2, *p3, k5; rep from * to last 3 sts, k3.

9th row: P8, T4L, *p4, T4L; rep from * to last st, p1.

10th row: K1, *p3, k5; rep from * to last 4 sts, k4.

11th row: P1, *T4L, p4; rep from * to last 4 sts, p4.

12th row: K8, p3, *k5, p3; rep from * to last 2 sts, k2.

13th row: P2, *T4L, p4; rep from * to last 3 sts, p3.

14th row: K7, p3, *k5, p3; rep from * to last 3 sts, k3.

15th row: P3, *T4L, p4; rep from * to last 2 sts, p2.

16th row: K6, p3, *k5, p3; rep from * to last 4 sts, k4.

Rep these 16 rows.

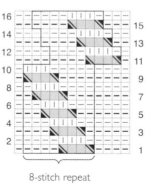

8-stitch repeat

5th row: K2, p2, [k1, p1] twice, k1, p2, k2.

6th row: P1, T3B, [k1, p1] twice, k1, T3F, p1.

7th row: K1, p2, [k1, p1] 3 times, k1, p2, k1.

8th row: T3B, [k1, p1] 3 times, k1, T3F.

9th row: P2, [k1, p1] 4 times, k1, p2.

10th row: T3F, [p1, k1] 3 times, p1, T3B.

11th row: K1, p2, [k1, p1] 3 times, k1, p2, k1.

12th row: P1, T3F, [p1, k1] twice, p1, T3B, p1.

13th row: As 5th row.

14th row: P2, T3F, p1, k1, p1, T3B, p2.

15th row: As 3rd row.

16th row: P3, T3F, p1, T3B, p3.

17th row: As 1st row.

18th row: P4, C5B, p4.

19th row: As 1st row.

20th row: P3, T3B, p1, T3F, p3.

21st row: [K3, p2] twice, k3.

22nd row: P2, T3B, p3, T3F, p2.

23rd row: K2, p2, k5, p2, k2.

24th row: P2, k2, p2, make bobble (MB) as follows: [k1, yf, k1, yf, k1] into next st, turn, p5, turn, k5, turn, p2tog, p1, p2tog, turn, sl 1, k2tog, psso (bobble completed), p2, k2, p2.

25th row: As 23rd row.

26th row: P2, T3F, p3, T3B, p2.

27th row: As 21st row.

28th row: P3, T3F, p1, T3B, p3.

29th row: As 1st row.

30th row: As 18th row.

Rep these 30 rows.

Moss and Bobble Cable

Panel of 13 sts on a background of reverse St st.

1st row (wrong side): K4, p2, k1, p2, k4.

2nd row: P3, T3B, k1, T3F, p3.

3rd row: K3, p2, k1, p1, k1, p2, k3.

4th row: P2, T3B, k1, p1, k1, T3F, p2.

Wave Cable

Panel of 6 sts on a background of reverse St st.

1st row (right side): Knit.

2nd row: Purl.

3rd row: C6B.

4th row: Purl.

5th to 8th rows: Work 1st and 2nd rows twice more.

9th row: C6F.

10th row: Purl.

11th and 12th rows: Work 1st and 2nd rows once more.

Rep these 12 rows.

Zig-Zag Cable II

Multiple of 6 + 2.

1st row (right side): P4, T3B, *p3, T3B; rep from * to last st, p1.

2nd row: K2, *p2, k4; rep from * to end.

3rd row: *P3, T3B; rep from * to last 2 sts, p2.

4th row: K3, p2, *k4, p2; rep from * to last 3 sts, k3.

5th row: P2, *T3B, p3; rep from * to end.

6th row: *K4, p2; rep from * to last 2 sts, k2.

7th row: P1, *T3B, p3; rep from * to last st, p1.

8th row: K5, p2, *k4, p2; rep from * to last st, k1.

9th row: P1, T3F, p3; rep from * to last st, p1.

10th row: As 6th row.

11th row: P2, *T3F, p3; rep from * to end.

12th row: As 4th row.

13th row: *P3, T3F; rep from * to last 2 sts, p2.

14th row: As 2nd row.

15th row: P4, T3F, *p3, T3F; rep from * to last st, p1.

16th row: K1, *p2, k4; rep from * to last st, k1.

Rep these 16 rows.

Note: The stitch is also very effective when worked as a panel of 8 or 14 sts on a background of reverse St st.

6-stitch repeat

Turning Diagonals

Multiple of 8 + 10.

1st row (right side): P3, k4, *p4, k4; rep from * to last 3 sts, p3.

2nd row: K3, p4, *k4, p4; rep from * to last 3 sts, k3.

3rd row: P3, C4B, *p4, C4B; rep from * to last 3 sts, p3.

4th row: As 2nd row.

5th to 8th rows: Rep the last 4 rows once more.

9th row: P1, *T4B, T4F; rep from * to last st, p1.

10th row: K1, p2, k4, *p4, k4; rep from * to last 3 sts, p2, k1.

11th row: P1, k2, p4, *C4F, p4, rep from * to last 3 sts, k2, p1.

12th row: As 10th row.

13th row: P1, *T4F, T4B; rep from * to last st, p1.

14th row: As 2nd row.

15th row: As 3rd row.

16th row: As 2nd row.

Rep these 16 rows.

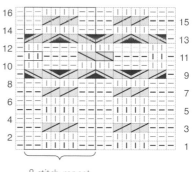

8-stitch repeat

Cable with Bobble Cluster

Panel of 11 sts on a background of reverse St st.

1st row (right side): P3, k2, MB#8, k2, p3.

2nd row: K3, p5, k3.

3rd row: P3, MB#8, k3, MB#8, p3.

4th row: K3, p5, k3.

5th and 6th rows: As 1st and 2nd rows.

7th row: P2, T3B, p1, T3F, p2.

8th row: K2, p2, k1, p1, k1, p2, k2.

9th row: P1, T3B, k1, p1, k1, T3F, p1.

10th row: K1, p3, k1, p1, k1, p3, k1.

11th row: T3B, p1, [k1, p1] twice, T3F.

12th row: P2, k1, [p1, k1] 3 times, p2.

13th row: K3, p1, [k1, p1] twice, k3.

14th row: As 12th row.

15th row: T3F, p1, [k1, p1] twice, T3B.

16th row: As 10th row.

17th row: P1, T3F, k1, p1, k1, T3B, p1.

18th row: As 8th row.

19th row: P2, T3F, p1, T3B, p2.

20th row: K3, p5, k3.

Rep these 20 rows.

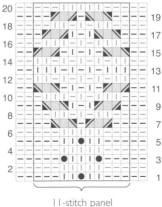

11-stitch panel

Fancy Trellis Cable

Panel of 22 sts on a background of reverse St st.

1st row (right side): K1, p2, k1, p3, k2, p4, k2, p3, k1, p2, k1.

2nd row: P1, k2, p1, k3, p2, k4, p2, k3, p1, k2, p1.

3rd row: T2F, T2B, p3, T3F, p2, T3B, p3, T2F, T2B.

4th row: K1, C2BW, k5, p2, k2, p2, k5, C2BW, k1.

5th row: T2B, T2F, p4, T3F, T3B, p4, T2B, T2F.

6th row: P1, k2, p1, k5, p4, k5, p1, k2, p1.

7th row: K1, p2, k1, p5, C4B, p5, k1, p2, k1.

8th row: As 6th row.

9th row: T2F, T2B, p3, C4B, C4F, p3, T2F, T2B.

10th row: K1, C2BW, k4, p8, k4, C2BW, k1.

11th row: P5, T4B, k4, T4F, p5.

12th row: K5, p2, k2, p4, k2, p2, k5.

13th row: P3, T4B, p2, C4B, p2, T4F, p3.

14th row: K3, p2, k4, p4, k4, p2, k3.

15th row: P1, T4B, p3, T3B, T3F, p3, T4F, p1.

16th row: K1, p2, k5, p2, k2, p2, k5, p2, k1.

17th row: T2B, T2F, p3, T3B, p2, T3F, p3, T2B, T2F.

18th row: As 2nd row.

Rep these 18 rows.

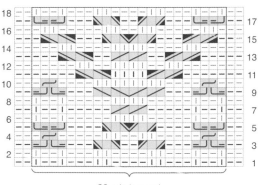

22-stitch panel

Honeycomb Cable

Panel of 12 sts on a background of reverse St st.

1st row (right side): K4, C2F, C2B, k4.

2nd and every alt row: Purl.

3rd row: K2, [C2F, C2B] twice, k2.

5th row: [C2F, C2B] 3 times.

7th row: [C2B, C2F] 3 times.

9th row: K2, [C2B, C2F] twice, k2.

11th row: K4, C2B, C2F, k4.

12th row: Purl.

Rep these 12 rows.

It is always a good idea to knit a gauge swatch before starting a project. Try different needle sizes until you get the correct gauge.

Elongated Cable Plait

Panel of 12 sts on a background of reverse St st.

1st row (wrong side): K3, p6, k3.

2nd row: P3, k2, C4B, p3.

3rd row: As 1st row.

4th row: P3, C4F, k2, p3.

5th to 9th rows: Rep the last 4 rows once more, then the 1st row again.

10th row: P2, T3B, k2, T3F, p2.

11th row: K2, p2, [k1, p2] twice, k2.

12th row: P1, T3B, p1, k2, p1, T3F, p1.

13th row: K1, [p2, k2] twice, p2, k1.

14th row: T3B, p2, k2, p2, T3F.

15th row: [P2, k3] twice, p2.

16th row: T3F, p2, k2, p2, T3B.

17th row: As 13th row.

18th row: P1, T3F, p1, k2, p1, T3B, p1.

19th row: As 15th row.

20th row: P2, T3F, k2, T3B, p2.

21st to 24th rows: Rep first 4 rows once more.

Rep these 24 rows.

Loops and Spirals

Multiple of 16 + 8.

1st row (right side): P2, C4B, *p4, C4B; rep from * to last 2 sts, p2.

2nd row: K2, p4, *k4, p4; rep from * to last 2 sts, k2.

3rd row: P2, k2, *T4F, T4B; rep from * to last 4 sts, k2, p2.

4th row: K2, p2, k2, p4, *k4, p4; rep from * to last 6 sts, k2, p2, k2.

5th row: P2, k2, p2, C4F, *p4, C4F; rep from * to last 6 sts, p2, k2, p2.

6th row: As 4th row.

7th row: P2, k2, *T4B, T4F; rep from * to last 4 sts, k2, p2.

8th row: As 2nd row.

9th and 10th rows: As 1st and 2nd rows.

11th row: P2, k4, *p2, T4B, T4F, p2, k4; rep from * to last 2 sts, p2.

12th row: K2, p4, k2, *p2, k4, p2, k2, p4, k2; rep from * to end.

13th row: P2, C4B, p2, *k2, p4, k2, p2, C4B, p2; rep from * to end.

14th row: As 12th row.

15th row: P2, k4, p2, *T4F, T4B, p2, k4, p2; rep from * to end.

16th row: As 2nd row.

Rep these 16 rows.

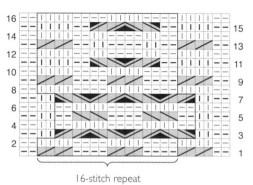

16-stitch repeat

Embedded Donuts I

Multiple of 16 + 10.

1st row (right side): K3, C4B, *k4, C4B; rep from * to last 3 sts, k3.

2nd and every alt row: Purl.

3rd row: K1, C4B, C4F, *k8, C4B, C4F; rep from * to last st, k1.

5th row: Knit.

7th row: K1, C4F, C4B, *k8, C4F, C4B; rep from * to last st, k1.

9th row: As 1st row.

11th row: K9, *C4B, C4F, k8; rep from * to last st, k1.

13th row: Knit.

15th row: K9, *C4F, C4B, k8; rep from * to last st, k1.

16th row: Purl.

Rep these 16 rows.

16-stitch repeat

Chain Cable

Panel of 9 sts on a background of reverse St st.

1st row (right side): P2, T5R, p2.

2nd row: K2, p2, k1, p2, k2.

3rd row: P1, T3B, p1, T3F, p1.

4th row: K1, p2, k3, p2, k1.

5th row: T3B, p3, T3F.

6th row: P2, k5, p2.

7th row: K2, p5, k2.

8th row: As 6th row.

9th row: T3F, p3, T3B.

10th row: As 4th row.

11th row: P1, T3F, p1, T3B, p1.

12th row: As 2nd row.

Rep these 12 rows.

Note: The cable as given above twists to the right. To work the cable twisted to the left, work T5L instead of T5R in the 1st row.

Diamonds with Spirals

Panel of 12 sts on a background of reverse St st.

1st row (right side): P4, k4, p4.

2nd row: K4, p4, k4.

3rd row: P4, C4B, p4.

4th row: K4, p4, k4.

5th row: P3, C3B, C3F, p3.

6th row: K3, p2, k2, p2, k3.

7th row: P2, C3B, k2, C3F, p2.

8th row: K2, p2, k4, p2, k2.

9th row: P1, C3B, k4, C3F, p1.

10th row: K1, p2, k6, p2, k1.

11th row: C3B, k6, C3F.

12th row: P2, k8, p2.

13th row: T3F, k6, T3B.

14th row: As 10th row.

15th row: P1, T3F, k4, T3B, p1.

16th row: As 8th row.

17th row: P2, T3F, k2, T3B, p2.

18th row: As 6th row.

19th row: P3, T3F, T3B, p3.

20th to 22nd rows: As 2nd to 4th rows.

Rep these 22 rows.

Medallion Cable

Panel of 13 sts on a background of reverse St st.

1st row (right side): Knit.

2nd row: Purl.

3rd and 4th rows: Rep the last 2 rows once more.

5th row: C6F, k1, C6B.

6th row: As 2nd row.

7th row: As 1st row.

8th to 11th rows: Rep the last 2 rows twice more.

12th row: As 2nd row.

13th row: C6B, k1, C6F.

14th row: As 2nd row.

15th row: As 1st row.

16th row: As 2nd row.

Rep these 16 rows.

9-Stitch Cable with Bobbles

Panel of 9 sts on a background of reverse St st.

1st row (right side): Knit.

2nd row: Purl.

3rd and 4th rows: Rep the last 2 rows once more.

5th row: C9F.

6th row: Purl.

7th row: K4, [k1, yf, k1, yf, k1] into next st, turn and k5, turn and p5, turn and sl 1, k1, psso, k1, k2tog, turn and p3tog (1 bobble completed), k4.

8th row: Purl.

9th to 12th rows: Rep 1st and 2nd rows twice more. Rep these 12 rows.

5th row: P2, T4R, k4, T4L, p2.

6th row: K2, p3, k1, p4, k1, p3, k2.

7th row: P1, T4R, p1, C4B, p1, T4L, p1.

8th row: K1, p3, k2, p4, k2, p3, k1.

9th row: T4R, p2, k4, p2, T4L.

10th row: P3, k3, p4, k3, p3.

11th row: K3, p3, C4B, p3, k3.

12th row: As 10th row.

13th row: T4L, p2, k4, p2, T4R.

14th row: As 8th row.

15th row: P1, T4L, p1, C4B, p1, T4R, p1.

16th row: As 6th row.

17th row: P2, T4L, k4, T4R, p2.

18th row: K3, p10, k3.

19th row: P3, T4L, k2, T4R, p3.

20th row: K4, p8, k4.

21st row: P4, T4L, T4R, p4.

22nd row: K5, p6, k5.

23rd row: P5, C6B, p5.

24th row: K5, p6, k5.

Rep these 24 rows.

Diamonds with Roses

Panel of 16 sts on a background of reverse St st.

1st row (right side): P4, C4R, C4L, p4.

2nd row: K4, p8, k4.

3rd row: P3, C4R, k2, C4L, p3.

4th row: K3, p10, k3.

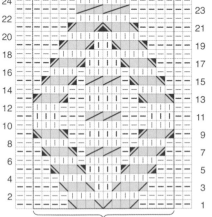

16-stitch panel

Alternating Diamonds

Multiple of 8 + 4.

1st row (right side): P5, C2B, *p6, C2B; rep from * to last 5 sts, p5.

2nd row: K5, p2, *k6, p2; rep from * to last 5 sts, k5.

3rd row: P4, *C2B, C2F, p4; rep from * to end.

4th row: K4, *p4, k4; rep from * to end.

5th row: P3, *C2B, k2, C2F, p2; rep from * to last st, p1.

6th row: K3, *p6, k2; rep from * to last st, k1.

7th row: P2, *C2B, k4, C2F; rep from * to last 2 sts, p2.

8th row: Purl.

9th row: K1, C2B, *k6, C2B; rep from * to last st, k1.

10th row: Purl.

11th row: P2, *T2F, k4, T2B; rep from * to last 2 sts, p2.

12th row: As 6th row.

13th row: P3, *T2F, k2, T2B, p2; rep from * to last st, p1.

14th row: As 4th row.

15th row: P4, *T2F, T2B, p4; rep from * to end.

16th row: As 2nd row.

Rep these 16 rows.

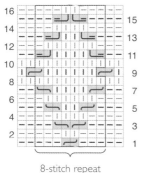

8-stitch repeat

Enclosed Cables

Panel of 14 sts on a background of reverse St st.

1st row (right side): P1, k2, p2, C4F, p2, k2, p1.

2nd row: K1, p2, k2, p4, k2, p2, k1.

3rd row: P1, k2, p2, k4, p2, k2, p1.

4th row: As 2nd row.

5th to 10th rows: Rep the last 4 rows once more, then the 1st and 2nd rows again.

11th row: P1, [T3F, T3B] twice, p1.

12th row: K2, [p4, k2] twice.

13th row: P2, [C4F, p2] twice.

14th row: As 12th row.

15th row: P1, [T3B, T3F] twice, p1.

16th row: As 2nd row.

17th row: As 1st row.

18th row: As 2nd row.

19th row: As 3rd row.

20th row: As 2nd row.

Rep these 20 rows.

Woven Diagonals

Multiple of 8 + 10.

1st row (right side): P3, C4B, *p4, C4B; rep from * to last 3 sts, p3.

2nd row: K3, p4, *k4, p4; rep from * to last 3 sts, k3.

3rd row: P1, *T4B, T4F; rep from * to last st, p1.

4th row: K1, p2, k4, *p4, k4; rep from * to last 3 sts, p2, k1.

5th row: P1, k2, p4, *C4F, p4; rep from * to last 3 sts, k2, p1.

6th row: As 4th row.

7th row: P1, *T4F, T4B; rep from * to last st, p1.

8th row: As 2nd row.

Rep these 8 rows.

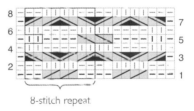

8-stitch repeat

Staghorn Cable

Panel of 16 sts on a background of reverse St st.

Foundation row: Purl.

1st row (right side): K4, CB4, C4F, k4.

2nd and 4th rows: Purl.

3rd row: K2, C4B, k4, C4F, k2.

5th row: C4B, k8, C4F.

6th row: Purl.

Rep these 6 rows.

Embedded Donuts II

Multiple of 18 + 10.

1st row (right side): Knit.

2nd row and every alt row: Purl.

3rd row: K1, C4B, C4F, *k10, C4B, C4F; rep from * to last st, k1.

5th row: Knit.

7th row: K1, C4F, C4B, *k10, C4F, C4B; rep from * to last st, k1.

9th row: Knit.

11th row: K10, *C4B, C4F, k10; rep from * to end.

13th row: Knit.

15th row: K10, *C4F, C4B, k10; rep from * to end.

16th row: Purl.

Rep these 16 rows.

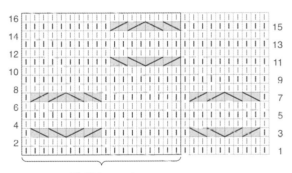

18-stitch repeat

8th row: K1, [p2, k1] 3 times.

9th row: P1, T3F, k2, T3B, p1.

10th row: K2, p6, k2.

11th row: P2, T3F, T3B, p2.

12th row: K3, p4, k3.

13th row: P3, C4F, p3.

14th row: K3, p4, k3.

15th row: P2, C3B, C3F, p2.

16th row: K2, p6, k2.

17th row: P1, T3B, k2, T3F, p1.

18th row: K1, [p2, k1] 3 times.

19th row: T3B, p1, k2, p1, T3F.

20th row: P2, [k2, p2] twice.

21st to 24th rows: Rep 1st and 2nd rows twice.

Rep these 24 rows.

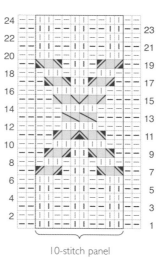

10-stitch panel

Cable with Central Stripe

Panel of 10 sts on a background of reverse St st.

1st row (right side): K2, [p2, k2] twice.

2nd row: P2, [k2, p2] twice.

3rd to 6th rows: Rep the last 2 rows twice more.

7th row: T3F, p1, k2, p1, T3B.

Braided Cable

Panel of 9 sts on a background of reverse St st.

1st row: T3F, T3B, T3F.

2nd row: P2, k2, p4, k1.

3rd row: P1, C4B, p2, k2.

4th row: As 2nd row.

5th row: T3B, T3F, T3B.

6th row: K1, p4, k2, p2.

7th row: K2, p2, C4F, p1.

8th row: As 6th row.

Rep these 8 rows.

Fancy Cross and Cable Panel

Panel of 24 sts on a background of reverse St st.

1st row (wrong side): [K2, p2] 3 times, [p2, k2] 3 times.

2nd row: P2, C2R, p2, T4F, C4F, T4B, p2, C2R, p2.

3rd row: K2, p2, k4, p8, k4, p2, k2.

4th row: P2, k2, p4, [C4B] twice, p4, k2, p2.

5th row: As 3rd row.

6th row: P2, C2R, p2, T4B, C4F, T4F, p2, C2R, p2.

7th row: [K2, p2] twice, k2, p4, [K2, p2] twice, k2.

8th row: P2, [k2, p2] twice, k4, p2, [k2, p2] twice.

9th row: K2, [p4, k4] twice, p4, k2.

10th row: P2, [k4, p4] twice, k4, p2.

11th row: As 9th row.

12th row: P2, k4, p4, C4F, p4, k4, p2.

13th row: As 9th row.

14th row: As 10th row.

15th row: As 9th row.

16th row: P2, k2, T4F, p2, k4, p2, T4B, k2, p2.

Rep these 16 rows.

Woven Lattice Cable

Panel of 13 sts on a background of reverse St st.

1st Foundation row (right side): Knit.

2nd Foundation row: Purl.

Rep the last 2 rows once more.

1st row: C6B, k1, C6F.

2nd row: Purl.

3rd row: Knit.

4th to 7th rows: Rep the last 2 rows twice more.

8th row: As 2nd row.

9th to 16th rows: Rep the last 8 rows once more.

17th row: C6F, k1, C6B.

18th row: As 2nd row.

19th row: As 3rd row.

20th to 23rd rows: Rep the last 2 rows twice more.

24th row: As 2nd row.

25th to 32nd rows: Rep the last 8 rows once more.

Rep these 32 rows.

key

C2B (Cross 2 Back) = slip next st onto cable needle and hold at back of work, knit st from left-hand needle, then knit st from cable needle.

C2BW (Cross 2 Back on Wrong Side) = slip next st onto cable needle and hold at back (right side) of work, purl next st from left-hand needle, then purl st from cable needle.

C2F (Cross 2 Front) = slip next st onto cable needle and hold at front of work, knit next st from left-hand needle, then knit st from cable needle.

C2FW (Cross 2 Front on Wrong Side) = slip next st onto cable needle and hold at front (wrong side) of work, purl next st from left-hand needle, then purl st from cable needle.

C3B (Cable 3 Back) = slip next st onto cable needle and hold at back of work, knit next 2 sts from left-hand needle, then knit st from cable needle.

C3F (Cable 3 Front) = slip next 2 sts onto cable needle and hold at front of work, knit next st from left-hand needle, then knit sts from cable needle.

C3L (Cable 3 Left) = slip next st onto cable needle and hold at back of work, knit next 2 sts from left-hand needle, then knit st from cable needle.

C3R (Cable 3 Right) = slip next 2 sts onto cable needle and hold at back of work, knit next st from left-hand needle, then knit sts from cable needle.

C4B (Cable 4 Back) = slip next 2 sts onto cable needle and hold at back of work, knit next 2 sts from left-hand needle, then knit sts from cable needle.

C4F (Cable 4 Front) = slip next 2 sts onto cable needle and hold at front of work, knit next 2 sts from left-hand needle, then knit sts from cable needle.

C4L (Cross 4 Left) = slip next 3 sts onto cable needle and hold at front of work, knit next st from left-hand needle, then knit sts from cable needle.

C4R (Cable 4 Right) = slip next st onto cable needle and hold at back of work, knit next 3 sts from left-hand needle, then knit st from cable needle.

C5B (Cable 5 Back) = slip next 3 sts onto cable needle and hold at back of work, knit next 2 sts from left-hand needle, then knit sts from cable needle.

C5F (Cable 5 Front) = slip next 2 sts onto cable needle and hold at front of work, knit next 3 sts from left-hand needle, then knit sts from cable needle.

C6B (Cable 6 Back) = slip next 3 sts onto cable needle and hold at back of work, knit next 3 sts from left-hand needle, then knit sts from cable needle.

C6F (Cable 6 Front) = slip next 3 sts onto cable needle and hold at front of work, knit next 3 sts from left-hand needle, then knit sts from cable needle.

C7B (Cable 7 Back) = slip next 4 sts onto cable needle and hold at back of work, knit next 3 sts from left-hand needle, then knit sts from cable needle.

C8B (Cable 8 Back) = slip next 4 sts onto cable needle and hold at back of work, knit next 4 sts from left-hand needle, then knit sts from cable needle.

C8F (Cable 8 Front) = slip next 4 sts onto cable needle and hold at front of work, knit next 4 sts from left-hand needle, then knit sts from cable needle.

C10B (Cable 10 Back) = slip next 5 sts onto cable needle and hold at back of work, knit next 5 sts from left-hand needle, then knit sts from cable needle.

C10F (Cable 10 Front) = slip next 5 sts onto cable needle and hold at front of work, knit next 5 sts from left-hand needle, then knit sts from cable needle.

C12B (Cable 12 Back) = slip next 6 sts onto cable needle and hold at back of work, knit next 6 sts from left-hand needle, then knit sts from cable needle.

C12F (Cable 12 Front) = slip next 6 sts onto cable needle and hold at front of work, knit next 6 sts from left-hand needle, then knit sts from cable needle.

MIK (Make 1 st knitwise) Pick up strand of yarn lying between last st worked and next st and knit into back of it.

MIP (Make 1st st purlwise) Pick up strand of yarn lying between last st worked and next st and purl into back of it.

M3 (Make 3 sts) [k1, p1, k1] all into next st on wrong-side rows.

T2BW (Twist 2 Back on wrong side) = Slip next st onto cable needle and hold at back (right side) of work, knit next st from left-hand needle, then purl st from cable needle.

T2B (Twist 2 Back) Slip next st onto cable needle and hold at back of work, knit next st from left-hand needle, then purl st from cable needle.

T2FW (Twist 2 Front on wrong side) = Slip next st onto cable needle and hold at front (wrong side) of work, purl next st from left-hand needle, then knit st from cable needle.

T2F (Twist 2 Front) Slip next st onto cable needle and hold at front of work, purl next st from left-hand needle, then knit st from cable nedle.

T6F (Twist 6 Front) = slip next 3 sts onto cable needle and hold at front of work, purl next 3 sts from left-hand needle, then knit sts from cable needle.

T3B (Twist 3 Back) = slip next st onto cable needle and hold at back of work, knit next 2 sts from left-hand needle, then purl st from cable needle.

T3F (Twist 3 Front) = slip next 2 sts onto cable needle and hold at front of work, purl next st from left-hand needle, then knit sts from cable needle.

T4BP (Twist 4 Back Purl) = slip next 2 sts onto cable needle and hold at back of work, knit next 2 sts from left-hand needle, then p1, k1 from cable needle.

T4B (Twist 4 Back) = slip next 2 sts onto cable needle and hold at back of work, knit next 2 sts from left-hand needle, then purl sts from cable needle.

T4FP (Twist 4 Front Purl) = slip next 2 sts onto cable needle and hold at front of work, k1, p1 from left-hand needle, then knit sts from cable needle.

T4F (Twist 4 Front) = slip next 2 sts onto cable needle and hold at front of work, purl next 2 sts from left-hand needle, then knit sts from cable needle.

T4L (Twist 4 Left) = slip next 3 sts onto cable needle and hold at front of work, purl next st from left-hand needle, then knit sts from cable needle

T4R (Twist 4 Right) = slip next st onto cable needle and hold at back of work, knit next 3 sts from left-hand needle, then purl st from cable needle.

T5BP (Twist 5 Back Purl) = slip next 3 sts onto cable needle and hold at back of work, knit next 2 sts from left-hand needle, then p1, k2 from cable needle.

T5B (Twist 5 Back) = slip next 3 sts onto cable needle and hold at back of work, knit next 2 sts from left-hand needle, then purl sts from cable needle.

T5F (Twist 5 Front) = slip next 2 sts onto cable needle and hold at front of work, purl next 2 sts from left-hand needle, then knit sts from cable needle.

T5L (Twist 5 Left) = slip next 3 sts onto cable needle and hold at front of work, purl next 2 sts from left-hand needle, then knit sts from cable needle.

T5R (Twist 5 Right) = slip next 2 sts onto cable needle and hold at back of work, knit next 3 sts from left-hand needle, then purl sts from cable needle.

T6B (Twist 6 Back) = slip next 3 sts onto cable needle and hold at back of work, knit next 3 sts from left-hand needle, then purl sts from cable needle.

Sl 1, k2tog, psso

Sl 1, k1, psso

Sl 2tog knitwise, k1, p2sso

⑤

Sl 1

Slip one st with yarn at back (wrong side) of work.

☒

PB1

purl into back of st on wrong side rows.

☑

KB1

Knit into back of st on right side rows.

⊟

P

Purl on right side rows.

⊞

P

Purl on wrong side rows.

◪

k2tog

Knit two together.

☑

PB1

Purl into back of st on wrong side rows.

☒

KB1

Knit into back of st on wrong side rows.

⊞

K

Knit on right side rows.

⊟

K

Knit on wrong side rows

☑

M3 (Make 3 sts)

[k1, p1, k1] all into next st.

◪

P2tog

◪

P3tog (on wrong side)

◪

P3tog

MB#1

(Make Bobble number 1)

(K1, p1) twice all into next st, pass 2nd, then 3rd and 4th sts over first st and off needle (bobble completed).

MB#2

(Make Bobble number 2)

(K1, p1) twice all into next st, turn and p4, turn and sl 2, k2tog, p2sso (bobble completed)

MB#3

(Make Bobble number 3)

(K1, p1) twice all into next st, turn and p4, turn and k4, turn and p4, turn and sl 2, k2tog, p2sso (bobble completed).

MB#4

(Make Bobble number 4)

(K1, p1) twice all into next st (turn and p4, turn and k4) twice, turn and p4, turn and sl 2, k2tog, p2sso (bobble completed)

MB#5

(Make Bobble number 5)

(K1, p1) twice all into next st, turn and k4, turn and sl 2, k2tog, p2sso (bobble completed)

MB#6

(Make Bobble number 6)

(K1, p1) twice all into next st, turn and k4, turn and p4, turn and k4, turn and sl 2, k2tog, p2sso (bobble completed)

MB #7

(Make Bobble number 7)

(K1, p1) twice all into next st, (turn and k4, turn and p4) twice, turn and k4, turn and sl 2, k2tog, p2sso (bobble completed)

MB#8

(Make Bobble number 8)

(K1, p1) three times all into next st, pass 2nd, then 3rd, 4th, 5th and 6th sts over first st and off needle (bobble completed)

MB#9

(Make Bobble number 9)

(K1, p1) three times all into next st, turn and p6, turn and sl 3, k3tog, p3sso st resulting from k3tog (bobble completed)

MB#10

(Make Bobble number 10)

(K1, p1) three times all into next st, turn and p6, turn and k6, turn and p6, turn and sl 3, k3tog, p3sso st resulting from k3tog (bobble completed)

MB#11

(Make Bobble number 11)

(K1, p1) three times all into next st, (turn and p6, turn and k6) twice, turn and p6, turn and sl 3, k3tog, p3sso st resulting from k3tog (bobble completed)

MB#12

(Make Bobble number 12)

(K1, p1) three times all into next st, turn and k6, turn and sl 3, k3tog, p3sso st resulting from k3tog (bobble completed)

MB#13

(Make Bobble number 13)

(K1, p1) three times all into next st, turn and k6, turn and p6, turn and k6, turn and sl 3, k3tog, p3sso resulting from k3tog (bobble completed)

MB#14

(Make Bobble number 14)

(K1, p1) three times all into next st, (turn and k6, turn and p6) twice, turn and k6, turn and sl 3, k3tog, p3sso st resulting from k3tog (bobble completed)

MB#15

(Make Bobble number 15)

Knit into front, back and front of next st, turn and k3, turn and p3, turn and k3, turn and sl 1, k2tog, psso (bobble completed)

abbreviations

[ ]	work instructions within brackets as many times as directed
* *	repeat instructions following the asterisks as directed
alt	alternate
C2B	cross 2 back; knit into back (or front) of 2nd st on needle, then knit first st, slipping both sts off needle at the same time.
C2BW	cross 2 back on wrong side; slip next st onto cable needle and hold at back (right side) of work, Purl next st from left-hand needle, then Purl next st from cable needle.
C2F	cross 2 front; knit into front of 2nd st on needle, then knit first st, slipping both sts off needle at the same time
C2FW	cross 2 front on wrong side; slip next st onto cable needle and hold at front (wrong side) of work, Purl next st from left-hand needle, then Purl st from cable needle.
C2L	cross 2 left; slip next st onto cable needle and hold at front of work, knit next St from left-hand needle, then knit st from cable needle.
C2LR	cross 2 left and right
C2R	cross 2 right; slip next st onto cable needle and hold at back of work, knit next st from left-hand needle, then knit st from cable needle.
C2tog	cross 2 together
C6 (Cross 6)	slip next 4 sts onto cable needle and hold at front of work, knit next 2 sts from left-hand needle, then slip the 2 purl sts from cable needle back to left-hand needle. Pass cable needle backwith 2 remaining knit sts to back of work, purl 2 sts from left-hand needle, then knit the 2 sts from cable needle.
cm	centimeter(s)
in	inch(es)

inc	increase
k	knit
k2tog	knit 2 together
K1B	knit 1 below (increase)
KB1	knit into back of next stitch
MB	make bobble
M1K	make 1 knit
M1P	make 1 purl
p	purl
p2tog	purl 2 together
PB1	purl into back of next stitch
psso	pass slip stitch over
rep	repeat(s)
RS	right side
sl	slip
St st	stockinette stitch
st(s)	stitch(es)
T2B	twist 2 back
T2BP	twist 2 back purl
T2BR	twist 2 back right
T5BR	twist 5 back right; slip next 3 sts onto cable needle and leave at back of work, knit next 2 sts from left-hand needle, then purl the 3 sts from cable needle.
T2F	twist 2 front
T2FL	twist 2 front left
T5FL	twist 5 front left; slip next 2 sts onto cable needle and hold at front of work, purl next 3 sts from left-hand needle, then knit the 2 sts from cable needle.
T2FP	twist 2 front purl
T2L	twist 2 left
T2R	twist 2 right
T2RP	twist 2 right purl
tbl	through back loop
tog	together
wyib	with yarn in back
wyif	with yarn in front
yb	yarn to the back
yf	yarn to the front
yfrn	with yarn in front

index

resources

Rowan

Westminster Fibers, Inc

3, Northern Boulevard

Suite 3

Amherst

NH 03031

www.westminsterfibers.com

Other titles currently available in the Harmony Guides series: